MW01274792

LIVING
WITH
YOURSELF

LIVING
WITH
YOURSELF

WHAT A MONK, AND FAITH, TAUGHT ME ABOUT MY MIND

BOBBY BASRAN

Clovercroft Publishing

Living with Yourself

©2020 by Bobby Singh Basran

Published by Clovercroft Publishing, Franklin, Tennessee.

www.clovercroftpublishing.com

Line edit by Erin McKnight

Copy edit by Jerome Ludwig

Editing by Kevin Anderson & Associates

Jacket design by Kevin Klover

Author photo by Anita Matharu

Cover and Interior Design by Adept Content Solutions

ISBN: 978-1-950892-78-5

Printed in the United States of America

*I dedicate this book to the two people
who impacted my life in ways that
will always be unforgettable:*

Ajahn Sona and Pastor Michael Todd

God's plan

—Drake

Contents

In loving memory of my
second mum Hardeep Matharu

September 28 1964–May 23 2020

I am so thankful I had the opportunity
to have you in my life. You will always
have a special place in my heart. I know
you are looking down on us every single
day and for that reason I am going to do
my absolute best to make you proud. I
love you and I will forever miss you.

Introduction

Wherever you go, there you are.

—Jon Kabat-Zinn

Your mind controls the entirety of your life to include how you act, how you treat people, how you see the world, and most importantly how you perceive your experiences. Many people think that if it is no good in this relationship, this city, this purpose, this house, this family, then in another relationship, city, purpose, house, or family, it will be better. Sometimes we can make a change and our lives will improve, but for the most part that does not work, because the problem does not rest in the external but rather in the internal, which is our mind. For instance, the problem is not your kids; it is your habit of constantly getting angry when you become frustrated. The problem is not your spouse; it is your inability to focus in the present moment. The problem is not where you live; it is your belief that an external factor will bring joy to your negative mind. The problem is not out there; it is in here—in your mind.

Wherever you go, there you are; meaning, you take along the one thing that shapes you, defines you, and never leaves you—your mind. If you get a new job, it will not cure your habit of always thinking that life is out to get you. If you obtain more money, it will not change the fact that you are a negative person. If you purchase a new house, it will not cure your urge to drink, steal, and cheat. You can have everything

1

you ever dreamed about, but if your undisciplined mind is in the habit of comparison, it will make you feel like you have nothing. You see, it is not about what we have or where we go, because we can have plenty and be in an amazing city with great people, but if our mind is undisciplined it will cast darkness all over our brightest achievements.

We work so hard to obtain this fairy-tale life, in which we have all the money in the world, fame, success, beautiful relationships, freedom, and so forth. All of these external factors are remarkable and important, but understand this: none of those things matter if your mind is not a beautiful place to live in. Financial freedom, doing something you love, helping people, blessing your family in ways they thought they would never experience, travelling, having healthy kids, loving yourself, and having love for your soulmate is important. I believe you need all of this to live a complete life, but none of it will matter if you don't have control over your mind, because you will not be able to relish any of these possessions or experiences if your mind is in charge of you.

What is the point of having millions of dollars in your account, if your undisciplined mind has thoughts you cannot control and that make you feel depressed? What is the point of having free time, if you can't even sit in a room by yourself with no distractions and find pleasure in the simple moments? What is the point of carrying out your day-to-day plans, if you allow other people and situations to have the power to change who you want to be? What is the point of working hard, if you cannot even rest at nighttime because you can never shut your mind off? What is the point of creating beautiful experiences for you and your loved ones, if your mind cannot even be in the present moment and enjoy the experience because it is in the habit of constantly worrying about the future? What is the point of life, if you need external possessions to sustain your happiness, joy, and peace, which causes you to only ever have temporary happiness? What is the point of life when the one thing that stays with you forever is causing you so much suffering?

In his book *Waking Up*, Sam Harris writes, "Every experience you ever had has been shaped by your mind. Every relationship is as good or as bad as it is because the mind is involved. If you are perpetually angry, depressed, confused and unloving or your attention is elsewhere, it won't matter how successful you become or who's in your life—you won't enjoy it." I am tired of seeing people fail to value their mind, and who think external factors will be enough for them to live an enjoyable life. I am tired of seeing people suffer every single day simply because they don't have control over their mind. I am tired of seeing people experience so many blessings in their life yet remain unhappy. I am tired of seeing people not being who they were called to be, by allowing other people and situations to dictate who they should be. I am tired of seeing people wake up every day just to create their own suffering and cause their reality to suffer as well. God put me on a path to learn from and confront my battles so I can come out on top not just for myself but to teach other people how to overcome the battles we face every day. Throughout this book I want to teach you how to make your mind a beautiful place to live in, so you can always have joy, happiness, and peace wherever you go, no matter what you're doing or what you may or may not have. I told you that your mind never leaves your side; it is the only thing that will always stay with you. If this is the case, wouldn't you want the one thing that never leaves you to bring you internal peace and joy? Listen to the Dalai Lama's words: "We don't need more money, we don't need greater success or fame, we don't need the perfect body or even the perfect mate—right now, at this very moment, we have a mind, which is all the basic equipment we need to achieve complete happiness."

I was fortunate enough to have a sit-down discussion with head monk, Ajahn Sona at Birken monastery. During our interview he told me that the Buddha holds happiness as the highest value. He then went on to explain that no one will truly be happy by chasing ordinary things. Money is not enough. A certain amount of wealth is a blessing but is not the highest blessing. The highest blessing is unshakable peace. Where no amount of circumstantial change will ever shake you of your capacity to remain well and in peace, it is nirvana—the highest blessing that doesn't allow anything or anyone to affect your state of being. It is the end of suffering in one's own mind. I found myself living in this nirvana state when I started to do these six things: deciding who I wanted to be, plucking my thoughts, living with clarity, living in a loving kindness state of being, finding pleasure in my simple moments, and most importantly having faith. When you learn do to these six things, it will not matter what you have, what you are going through, or where you go, because I truly believe we live in our minds first and in reality second, which means our reality is a projection of what is taking place in our mind at every given moment. Therefore, no matter what is happening in our reality, as long as we make our mind a beautiful place to live in by following those six simple steps, we will be able to live with peace, happiness, and joy in every moment, because life is way too short and unpredictable to be lived any other way. This is why I wrote this book; I hope it impacts your life as much as writing it did mine. Thank you and enjoy!

CHAPTER I

Defining Who You Want to Be

The man that masters himself through self-discipline
can never be mastered by others.

—Napoleon Hill

Your state of being is who you are as a person; it is how you act, react, think, speak, carry yourself and how you treat others. We all have a state(s) of being. Some of us have an angry state, an insecure state, a judgmental state, a lustful state, an anxious state, a negative state, and so forth. Over time, through unconscious behavior and repetition, we create natural states of being for ourselves. This means that we act, react, think, speak, carry ourselves, and treat others not necessarily how we *want* to, but more in line with how we are *used* to doing.

My own state(s) of being were aggression, lust, and judgement. I would wake up every single day and act out of lust, anger, judgement, and frustration. I would watch porn every single day—multiple times per day, in fact—and I would always feel the need to be angry and see the worst in everything. I also had a massive ego, which caused me to judge people as if by second nature. As I continued to act in this manner, it slowly shifted to become my natural state of being.

Like many of you may feel today, I didn't want to act in these states, but through unconscious and habitual actions this became who I was.

Joe Dispenza a well-known neuroscientist, who has written several successful books including the best seller *Evolve Your Brain,* writes that "90% to 95% of who we are by the time we're 35 years old sits in a subconscious memory system in which most of our habits and behaviors exist." This means that who we practice being every day is the person we will automatically become when we are thirty-five years old. The way you express anger when people and situations get on your nerves will remain the same if you do not become conscious of this habitual behavior. The way you clutter your mind with thoughts that create stress, worry, and anxiety will become a habit that remains with you for the rest of your life. To put it simply, a habit happens when your body automatically responds and doesn't need the involvement of your mind. In other words, habit is when you do something so many times that your body comes to know how to do it better than your mind. In order to break any habit related to how you act, think, react, speak, or interpret things, you must become mindful of those things.

As for myself I was on pace to live the rest of my life as a porn-addicted, judgmental, incessantly worried, and aggressive person. I didn't want to watch porn; I didn't want to judge other people; I didn't want to be negative and see the worst in everything—but I continued to do so because over time I had created the habit of living unconsciously and doing what is easy. By never being mindful over the way I reacted, I unconsciously allowed other people and situations to have the power to change me. Just like many of you, I had been *created* as a person who I didn't want to be, and I would have continued to be this unhappy person had it not been for a life-changing experience.

In July of the 2019 summer, my older brother and I attended a beginners retreat at a monastery located in the outskirts of Kamloops, British Columbia. This particular monastery was a thirty-minute drive from where we actually live. The reason we decided to go on this retreat was to learn to live with ourselves in a more peaceful, happier and joyful manner.

When I arrived at the monastery, I took a seat on a bench that faced the vast wilderness. As I sat outside, and although I still struggle to roll the feelings I experienced into words, I felt as if the energy in the air was *vibrant*. The bugs around me caused me no harm; it simply felt as if the bugs were feeding off the monastery's and my own radiant energy.

During my stay at the monastery, I would come to meet a man who would change my way of living. His name is Ajahn Sona, and for the past thirty years he has been a practicing monk. The first lesson I learned at the monastery was to live based on how you wanted to live.

After I left the monastery and arrived home, I would sit in solitude and try to be conscious over the person I was acting like. This led me to realize that I actually hated who I was as a person. I realized this person was not who I wanted to be. So, I pulled out a piece of paper and asked myself, *who do I want to be in ten years? How do I want to act, how do I want to think, how do I want to react? How do I want to interpret things? How do I want to respond to negative people? How do I want to react to tough situations? How do I want to think when I am bored? How do I want to treat my spouse, kids, brothers, and family? How do I want to be perceived? How do I want to see the world? How do I want my mood and energy to be? How do I want my state of being to be?*

- I want to be present in all my experiences.
- I don't want to have any stress or worry.
- I want to speak about things that I value. Quality over quantity. Speak only when I have/want to; otherwise, I want to just sit and be quiet with a smile on my face.
- I don't want to suffer, since there is no suffering; there are only thoughts that create suffering.
- I want to consistently pluck my thoughts, which would allow me to replace the bad ones with good ones. Eventually, I will have only good thoughts to choose from when my mind decides to wander.
- I want to slow down and still be myself, no matter how fast-paced my day.
- I want to be filled with so much happiness, kindness, and love that I don't judge any other person or situation and instead simply continue to be me and wish the best for all things.
- I want to be in a loving and kind state of being at all times.
- I want to walk around with a free mind, looking at everything and anything for what they are and not what my thoughts think they are. I want to have a clear headspace. I want clarity.
- I want to be conscious over my mind at all times.
- I don't want to judge people, be jealous of people, or wish badly for people.
- I don't want to give people or situations the power to change my thoughts or actions.

- I don't want to act out of the character God called me to be in.
- I don't want to have constant lustful thoughts about women. This prohibits me from seeing women for who they are, rather than what my sexual mind sees them as.
- I want to have meaningful thoughts, thoughts that I value and that help me to become a better person.
- I want to respond to people based on who I am, not who they are. For example, if someone is being mean or annoying, I still want to be happy, kind, and loving, and have clarity. I don't want to stoop down to their level. I just want to continue to be me, despite any obstacles.
- I want to be calm every single day, with a smile on my face.
- I don't want to have excessive thinking about the past or the future. I simply want to be in the now, and have valuable thoughts of happiness, lovingness, kindness, and clarity.
- I want to ground my mind by focusing on my breath multiple times a day.

I followed this self-reflection with the Joe Dispenza theory that we create our future selves today through our daily habits, and wrote, *you are creating your future self today. How you act today is how you will act in the future. Same goes for the way you think, relate, and react to things. You are building habits every day through repetition and patterns. Who you are and how you act today will one day be your future self. React based on you, have valuable thoughts, relate to things in a meaningful way, and*

9

be your happy, loving, conscious, kind self, no matter the people or situations at hand.

I share this exercise with you because it is the very exercise that helped me to overcome my former undesirable state(s) of being. All of us have natural states—whether the state of fear, anger, lustfulness, victimization, insecurity, greed, ego, and so on—that we unconsciously act from. Allow me to help you better yourself. Pull out a piece of paper right now and do the exercise that changed my life and helped me make my mind a beautiful place to live in so that I could comfortably live with myself. Write down who you want to be, the type of everyday thoughts you wish to have, how you want to treat people, how you want to react to situations that you cannot control, how you want to react to people who are rude, and how you want to react to people who don't understand you. How do you want to act every single day? Like many of us, I was not mindful. However, I changed by understanding the importance of being mindful and by understanding Joe Dispenza's theory that we're creating who we are through our habits, patterns, and repetitions, and one future day this is who we are going to be. I changed by looking at who I want to be when I am thirty-five and have a family to take care of, and asked myself: *Do you really want to watch porn every single day? Do you really want to yell at your kids because you didn't practice controlling your emotions when you were younger? Do you really want to give people and situations the power to change your mood, emotions, and energy? Do you really want to live in a world where you have no control over your thoughts, which will lead you to have no control over how you act?*

When you write down exactly the person you wish to be, leave no stone unturned. Truly ask yourself and answer honestly: *How do I want to live this one life? How do I want my mood to be, every single day? How do I want my energy to be? How do I want to treat the people I love? How do I want to treat myself? How do I want to get up every morning? How do I want to go to bed every night? What thoughts do I want to think?*

Sit down and, by completing this exercise, define who you want to be and what state(s) of being you want to live in. It is quite simple: we live in two states and only in two states. The first state is that of suffering. Herein reside the sub states of anger, frustration—which manifests in feeling annoyed and is caused by having a state of ego—validation, self-importance, resentment—that is, feeling unfairly treated or living in a constant state of expectations or of living in the past—negativity, future-mindedness—which is evident in anxiety, stress, and worry. The second state, and the state we should all strive to live in, is the non-suffering state; the sub states includes the states of happiness, gratitude, clarity—embodied in the understanding of and appreciation for the present moment and in the state of positivity—and loving kindness.

People live in the first state and not in the second because we allow ourselves to be unconsciously and consciously affected by external factors such as people and situations, which eventually becomes a hard-to-break habit. Having to practice acting this way over and over until it becomes second nature to us should not be the case! We should live in a consistent state regardless of external factors. We should be living in a state that we choose to live in every day, despite what takes place in our life. The only way to achieve this, however, is by living every day with awareness over ourselves.

If it took consistent repetition to create the person we are now and the state(s) of being we act from, then it will take the same to create the new person we wish to become. Until the body and mind adapt to the habit of acting naturally in this manner, we need to consistently *act* as our new selves. For instance, if you are in the habit of reacting with anger when you're frustrated, annoyed, or as a general predisposition and you don't want to react in this manner anymore, you must become mindful of this reaction. Every single time, you have the ability to act as your old self by reacting with anger; you also have the ability to choose to be mindful of how this habit will eventually create your future self and you can respond differently and break the habit of reacting with anger. When you find yourself caught in a situation, consciously say to yourself, *I do not want to act like this, because when I do, I'm creating lifelong habits.* You determine who you want to be, and through self-discipline you start acting as that person. Just like habit created the old you, habit can create the new you. The goal is to live a life wherein you are being your true self no matter what's going on around you; the only way to do this is by practicing who you want to be until that person becomes your natural self.

In the beginning, there will be two of you: the person you want to become and the old you. The one you continue to act like will grow, while the other one will diminish. Have the consciousness to live your life by being yourself! Get into the habit of understanding that by practicing constant awareness over yourself, you are every day creating your future self. If you don't like the person you are today, mindfully start acting as who you want to be tomorrow. Do this by reminding yourself every day to be who you want to be, the way you consistently act will turn into who you are—your state(s) of being—which will continue to be who you are . . . until you decide to live mindfully by reprogramming the inner workings of your mind. When you free yourself from your old self by being mindful, you will discover that the work of mindfulness is waking up vitality in every moment that we have. Every moment that transpires in your life, be mindful by being alert. When you are alert in your moments, you can consciously remind yourself to be the person you wish to become.

When we become mindful of ourselves, we wield the power to never be controlled by others. When you are yourself despite external situations and other people, you practice great power: the power to live how *you* want to live. We suffer badly when we allow other people to dictate our moods and energy. By giving people the power to dictate or change who we want to be, we suffer from allowing a situation to get the better of us and in turn react with anger, frustration, and ego. We suffer when we allow ourselves to be controlled by external factors—so why allow it? Why permit a sense of power so strong and meaningful to someone or something other than yourself? Do you really want to live as a victim and allow yourself to be controlled? The moment doesn't matter; neither does the severity of the situation or what the other person did. Through it all, by continuing to be yourself you're teaching yourself that no one or no thing has the power to change you. This is important because throughout your life there are going to be many tough situations and many negative people who don't agree with you or don't see life the way you do. Are you really going to give those situations and people the power to determine who you are and who you want to be? Your state(s) of being shouldn't be determined by how other people act or the severity of the situation, but instead by who you are as a person and who you continually want to become.

I was truly not happy living unconsciously as a result of my habits. I hated myself and couldn't live with myself as this person. Many of you may know what it's like to feel this way. You're not at peace with yourself because you are not being yourself; instead, you're just being a person who is easy to be. You don't want to be a negative, greedy, self-centered, fearful, or insecure person, but you are one because you are living unconsciously. I have been there, living the way of an unconscious person, and I *hated* my life.

This self-discipline to be yourself gives you the power to be your true self. Because of this, you will be at peace—your mind will be a beautiful place. You will be able to sit alone with nothing but your mind and still be happy, because you are constantly being the person you want to be.

What I am trying to teach throughout this book, and in this section in particular, is that these principles are tools that create happiness, joy, and peace within yourself. These are tools that money, fame, and success cannot buy. This is the tool of self-discipline and mindfulness, which provides everlasting happiness and peace within yourself. How many times a day do we let a phone call ruin our mood? How often do we let a situation we cannot control impact our energy? How many times a day do we let another person dictate our happiness, our joy, our peace? You can have all the money in the world, healthy kids, a successful business, book deals, fame, and so forth, but if you continuously live as a victim of your mind by exercising no control over who you want to be, you will never be truly happy. Please listen to what the monk said to me: "The highest blessing is unshakable peace, where no amount of circumstantial change will ever shake your capacity to remain well and in peace."

It's time to stop suffering in your mind, and instead to make your mind a beautiful place in which to reside. This is achieved by practicing your ability to be who you want to be. The person who said it the best: Canadian rap icon Drake when he said, "You know it's real when you are who you think you are." Define who you want to be and be that person! People and situations will try to tear you down because that's life—unpredictable and unfair. But, if you have the awareness to define who you want to be and continue to be that person through having discipline, then nothing will ever *shake your capacity to remain well and in peace.*

CHAPTER 2

Plucking Your Thoughts

The happiness of your life, depends on the quality of your thoughts.

—Marcus Aurelius

Ajahn told me the two best states of being to live in are clarity and loving kindness. Clarity is when you see things for what they truly are, by not having thoughts affecting what you see, it is when you feel peace and silence on your mind. Loving kindness occur when you see the good in every person and situation; it happens when you have a smile on your face and exhibit a lack of ego. Ajahn continued to tell me that he had been living in these exact two states for thirty years, and they were the key to his joy, happiness, and peace. He said there is no better way to live. I thought about this for a moment and then asked him why more people didn't live in these states, if they are proven to create such amazing results? Ajahn's response: their level of undisciplined thinking wouldn't allow them to be in these states.

We have eighty thousand thoughts a day. That's three thousand three hundred thirty-three thoughts per hour, and fifty-five thoughts per minute. If you don't believe me, close your eyes this very second and focus on your breath by inhaling and exhaling through your nose for three minutes.

17

As many of you may notice when your mind is rested and focused on your breath going in and out of your nose, you begin to notice the flurry of thoughts racing through your mind. These thoughts are always roaming in our minds, but it is our ability to constantly keep ourselves distracted and our inability to have awareness over our minds that prevents us from noticing them.

People may win in the short-term by paying no attention to their thoughts, but these people are unaware of how these thoughts affect how they feel and act. Right this second, if you had a thought about your mother dying, for example, you would start to feel sad. Once you felt sad, your actions would soon start to match and you would carry yourself in a different manner, your facial expression would change, and your energy levels would drop. All this could originate with one single thought. This is just how one thought out of the fifty-five we have per minute has the potential to draw us out of our state of being if we continue to remain unconscious over our level of thinking.

During my time at the monastery I read a line in a book called *The Four Noble Truths*. The line read, "If I pull your fingernail off that is pain, what you do after is suffering." Reading this line helped me understand the notion that suffering is created through your mind. Suffering is how you constantly think about the pain. Many of us do this in our own lives every single day. The pain was the divorce, but the suffering was thinking about the situation daily. The pain was finding out that you have a disease, however the suffering was dwelling on the idea of not getting any better. You see, we as human beings don't need to suffer, because there is no suffering there are only thoughts that create suffering. Listen to the Buddha, who said, "Pain is certain, suffering is optional." The reason suffering is optional is because if we just have the self-discipline to remain aware of our thoughts, our suffering will not be created. We need to stop living mindlessly and understand that we do indeed have eighty thousand thoughts per day. Yes, we have three thousand three hundred thirty-three thoughts per hour. Fifty-five thoughts per minute! And these racing, uncontrollable thoughts have the ability to cause us to suffer immensely unless we understand Joe Dispenza's theory that "How you think is how you feel and how you feel is how you act." When we finally agree and understand this, we are only left with one question: How do we ensure our level of thinking does not cause us suffering?

Ajahn taught me the importance of having mastery over my level of thinking. He told me that when we obtain mastery over our thoughts, we have the discipline to be like the Buddha in the sense that we also have two groups of thoughts:

1. Unwholesome thoughts, or those thoughts we don't want to have
2. The thoughts we do want to have

The Buddha became a master of his thoughts by living this principle: "Whatever I wish to think that I think, whatever I don't wish to think that I do not think." Allow this passage to seep into and bathe your mind.

We humans think far too much and fail to realize that there is a time and place for thinking itself. We believe that if we think about our money problems, those money problems will be solved. We fail to realize that thinking alone never solves the problem—only action does. Yet we continue to think until we push ourselves into a state of stress and panic caused by this very thinking! This is just one example of thousands of thinking about things that we don't wish to think about. Imagine if we had this type of control in our everyday life—the wherewithal to think about things we actually want to think about and to not think about the things that cause us discomfort. Imagine if we were in control of the one thing that controlled us; we would no doubt suffer far less and create much more joy, happiness, and peace in our existence.

Ajahn truly believes everyone can become masters over their level of thinking. To do so, he said, you must become mindful over your mind and treat your mind as if it were a garden wherein the weeds are the thoughts you don't want to have and the flowers are the thoughts you wish to have. Ajahn went on to explain that your garden should never have more weeds than flowers because if you were to have more weeds than flowers, your garden would not be a beautiful place to be in.

The British philosophical writer James Allen, well known for his famous book *As a Man Thinketh* once said, "Every thought-seed sown or allowed to fall into the mind and to take root there produces its own, blossoming sooner or later into act." Before we allow our thoughts to take root in our mind, we can do the first step of the gardening method: prevention. Any time you have a thought you don't want to have, dismiss it before the thought lives its purpose by affecting how you feel and act. This requires you to be extremely mindful over the thoughts that occur in your mind, dismissing the thought before it impacts how you feel and act. A thought with no attention paid to it is simply a thought, and one that has no power. You are not your thoughts, and you should never think you are; your thoughts truly have a mind of their own. Therefore, the first step is simple: be observant of your mind. If you have an unwanted thought, prevent it from surfacing by simply shutting it down before you give your unconscious attention to it. Whatever you concentrate on, you give energy to. Ralph Waldo Emerson once said, "The only thing that can grow is the thing you give energy to." Before you give the thought you don't wish to have the energy to be activated, simply dismiss it. The way I dismiss a thought is by asking myself: *Do I really want to have this thought? Is this a thought based on who I want to be? Is this thought making my mood and energy better or worse? Is this thought making me feel happy? Or is this thought making me feel worried, stressed, fearful, and unhappy?*

Once you answer these questions for yourself, you will know whether or not to give your attention to the thought in question.

This method of dismissal is only the first step, because it doesn't work for all thoughts because all thoughts are not created equal. Many thoughts are stronger than others. Just like how a weed can get stronger with sunlight and water, the same can happen to your thoughts. The only difference is your thoughts become stronger with your attention and repetition. If you have thoughts that you try to dismiss, only to have them return, those thoughts are powerful and only dismissible by being replaced with other thoughts. This is the second step of the gardening method: removal and planting. We use the technique of removal and planting when we have repetitive thoughts that keep coming back into our mind. These are the thoughts that take you out of your state(s) of being and are the ones that are uncontrollable and focus on lust, judgement, anger, ego, fear, and so forth. These are the thoughts that you

21

don't want in your mind, but they endure there because you don't know how to get rid of them. Ajahn said these thoughts are based on the Buddhist tradition of the Five Hindrances, which are identified as mental factors that hinder progress in meditation and also in our daily lives, and include:

1. Sensory desire: The particular type of wanting that seeks happiness through the senses of sight, sound, smell, taste, and physical feeling. These are external factors for happiness, and include lust, greed, and wealth.
2. Ill will: Any thought related to wanting to reject, and includes feelings of hostility, resentment, hatred, and bitterness.
3. Sloth and Torpor: Heaviness of body and dullness of mind, which drag one down into disabling inertia and thick depression.
4. Restlessness and Worry: The inability to calm the mind.
5. Doubt, uncertainty, fear, lack of conviction or trust.

James Allen wrote "just as a gardener cultivates his plot, keeping it free from the weeds and growing the flowers and fruits which he requires, so may a man tend the garden of his mind, weeding out all the wrong, useless, and impure thoughts, and cultivating toward perfection the flowers and fruits of right, useful, and pure thoughts."

During our evening sit-down talk at the monastery, Ajahn asserted that every time we have a thought based on one of the hindrances, we need to pluck out the weed and replace it with a flower.

He said, "Imagine your mind as if it were a garden. When you have a thought that you don't wish to have, visualize plucking it out of your mind. Once you do this, plant the thought you want to replace it with as the flower." Over time, as you continue to practice this plucking method, you will begin to get into the habit of plucking every thought that causes you anything other than peace, happiness, and joy. Anytime you feel overwhelmed, stressed, fearful, not at peace, or not like yourself, you will automatically remember that you must be feeling this way because of a thought that is in your mind. Check back with your mind and see what it is thinking about, consciously address that thought, and then simply pluck the thought that is causing your suffering. When you do this exercise of removal and planting, you are giving attention to the thought that actually makes you feel at peace, happy, and joyful, instead of the thought that causes you pain, anger, and sadness.

HINDRANCES	OPPOSITES
1. Lust—wanting.	1. Giving.
2. Ill will—anger, frustration, ego.	2. Loving kindness.
3. Sloth or torpor—not being at peace.	3. Feeling at peace with yourself.
4. Stress/worry—an inability to calm your mind.	4. Relaxation—being present and having faith.
5. Lack of trust—feeling insecure.	5. Having faith/certainty/trust.

In the table to your left, you can see the hindrances and the opposite version of those thoughts. The following is a real-world example of how you remove and plant.

Let's say you are scrolling through Instagram and you see a post from one of your friends about how their business is thriving, and you think to yourself: *They don't deserve that success; I do. I work so much harder, so I should be the one to have that success—not them.* You may not know because you are not mindful over your mind, but the second you have this thought you've been pulled out of your state of being and have started to have negative energy within yourself. If you consider this thought, you will recognize that it is the second hindrance: Ill will. Having this thought does nothing to affect the outcome. Allow me to explain. If you simply think about how you deserve success over your friend, this level of thinking is not going to slow down your friend's success nor is it going to speed up yours. The only thing that this thinking will achieve is to make you carry negative energy within yourself. However, if we replace that hindering thought with the opposite, which is loving kindness, and you think to yourself, *I hope he continues to have success—he truly deserves it,* this thought likewise does nothing to affect the outcome, but it does allow you to be filled with positive energy over negative energy and it removes your ego by allowing you to honestly convey your wish for the success of someone other than yourself.

Another example is, imagine constantly focusing your attention on the thought of, *What if my purpose never turns into reality?* Throughout the day or even over weeks, you wouldn't be able to find peace, and would constantly feel worried and stressed, which would cause you to feel unhappy and unable to find any pleasure in your simple moments. But imagine if you were only aware of that thought and quickly replaced it with thought of, *I have faith my purpose will come into being.* Just by having this thought alone, your entire aura shifts into one of happiness, energy, calmness, and confidence.

Conversely, visualize yourself having constant thoughts of, *I am so tired; I have a headache and feel so weak.* (This is an example of the third hindrance of Sloth and Torpor.) Just by having these thoughts, you will begin to transform words into an emotion which in turn will become an action. You will begin to move slower, feel sorry for yourself, expect others to feel sorry for you, be increasingly negative, and carry this malignant energy around with you wherever you go. But now visualize yourself having the thoughts of, *I am healthy, I am at peace, and I feel great.* By having these thoughts instead of the first ones, you will have better energy and will feel much better within yourself.

Picture yourself walking down the street and noticing a person who is dressed and acting in an entirely different fashion than you ever would. You may think to yourself, *I hate people like this; they're so stupid.* I guarantee you the minute you have this thought, your entire facial expression would change. You would be likely to become angry, which would prevent you from being at peace. Now picture yourself seeing this person and thinking to yourself, *I love how people can be themselves; I hope he is truly happy.* Right there, in that moment, you would be likely to have a smile on your face and would feel at peace. Imagine how happy and positive you would feel with this thought running through your mind as opposed to the first one.

These are just four thoughts out of the eighty thousand we have every day. Imagine how many other thoughts act as mental hindrances. You do not need to feel like you are a horrible person for having these thoughts; I had all of these thoughts, along with many more. All you need to remember is that these thoughts are not you; they are just your unconscious ego-driven habits. Using this method of removing and planting, we have the capability to shatter this habit into tiny nonworkable pieces. Start by simply noticing that you actually have thoughts that have the capacity to cause you to feel and act. This is hard for people to grasp, because most people think they have no thoughts. The reason people don't think they have any thoughts is simply because they are not conscious of their own mind. Although you have eighty thousand thoughts rippling back and forth across your mind and pounding on each side of your head, the reason you may not think you do is because you live with no control over yourself. Sometimes you're happy. Sometimes you're sad. Other times, you're frustrated or angry. But we know that our thoughts control our emotions. For instance, if you are in a grocery store and you don't feel you have your keys or phone with you, why do you panic? You panic because you think that you have lost your items. Therefore, thoughts create emotions and emotions create the way we act. Many of us live like this every day out of the habit of being a different self every moment, due to living based on our unconscious thoughts. Pay attention to the thoughts that make you feel and act in ways that you don't value. Just as we define who we want to be, we need to define what type of thoughts we want to have—because these thoughts will create the person you become, whether you want to be that person or not. When you have a thought that is not compatible with who you want to be or how you want to act, follow the removal and planting method. Simply imagine how free you would feel when you had a thought of anger and you showed mindfulness by noticing it and replacing it with loving kindness. That thought of anger could have made you feel angry or frustrated for hours, but when you replace that thought you could instead feel loving kindness. The goal here is simple: to experience peace instead of suffering throughout our days. We can reach this goal by showing a level of consciousness and capability by plucking the thoughts that don't make us feel peaceful, happy, and joyful.

You don't want to be sitting at work and feeling stressed out because of the argument you had with your partner the night before. You don't want to be hanging out with your loved ones and feeling frustrated and angry over something your boss said three hours before. You don't want to be trying to find pleasure in the simple moments but being unable to because your thoughts won't allow it. Think about how many times we got pulled out of the state of being we want to be in because we had a single thought. Think about how many moments we felt angry, upset, nervous, or fearful throughout the days, weeks, months, and years all because we allowed these weeds to grow in our garden. Think about how many times we wanted to find pleasure in our simple moments, yet our uncontrollable thoughts didn't allow us to do so. Think about how many times you tried to go to bed, but your thoughts prevented you from doing so because they wanted to create anxiety by causing you to think about the worst possible things that could happen. Think about how many times you couldn't be present in your moments because your thoughts were in the past or in the future. Think about how many times you mistreated people, and even yourself, all because of your thoughts at the time.

27

I write with passion about this because it happened to me. At times I could not go to bed because my thoughts were creating anxiety by causing me to constantly think, *when is my success going to come? Are people going to buy my books? Are people going to listen to my podcast?* There have been countless times when I would be watching a movie and my mind wouldn't allow me to concentrate because my subconscious thoughts were telling me go scroll through hours of porn. There have been endless times when I couldn't even enjoy the simple moments of going to dinner with my girlfriend or playing basketball because my thoughts were creating stress by causing me to think about a situation that I had no control over. There have been so many times when I acted rudely, negatively, and aggressively toward people because my thoughts were creating an emotion, which then turned into an action. Our thoughts take so much from us, and they will continue to do so unless we are willing to change.

When I am not in a state of being of happiness, love, kindness, or clarity, I ask myself, *where is my mind right now?* Every time I ask myself this question, my thinking always draws me away from the state(s) of being I do not want to be in. Always question the things that are on your mind! Ask yourself, *why am I feeling worried, why can't I feel clarity, why am I not happy?* Chances are your thoughts are causing you to be out of alignment with who you want to be. Every time I have a thought that I know is causing me to feel anything other than loving kindness, I close my eyes and follow the above steps. When I do so, that negative thought has no power over me because I removed it before I gave it the only thing that makes it grow—attention. This is a superpower! Every time you don't feel like the person you want to be, you have the awareness to close your eyes and replace that thought with a better one. However, your mind is very smart and the more you do this, the more it will keep throwing the same thought at you. Your job is to not become frustrated; it is simply to continue to replace the thought and focus your attention on the flower rather than on the weed. Over time, through repetition and habit, we will begin to have control over our thoughts and thus finally allow ourselves control over who we want to be.

I lived unconsciously and without control over my thoughts until one day I asked myself: *If no change has transpired in my day-to-day life, how do I have good days and bad? If I wake up and am still living the exact same way I was living before, why am I happy one day and then angry the next? Why am I at peace one moment, then frustrated the next?* It is all because of our thinking. If we concentrate on our thoughts based on the hindrances (weeds), they will continue to grow stronger and stronger. However, if we have the ability to become mindful at all times, we can pluck the hindrances before they affect how we feel and act.

We cannot stop ourselves from thinking; thinking is what the mind does naturally, but we can change our thinking. Just imagine how much better our lives would be if we had thoughts based on the opposite of our hindrances. We would have fewer thoughts of lust, anger, tiredness, stress, worry, and disbelief, and more thoughts of giving, loving kindness, peacefulness, faith, belief, etc.

Too many times, our thoughts rob us of our joy, tranquility, happiness, peace, and even our experiences. Too many times, our thoughts cause us to live in a realm of utter darkness. Too many times, our thoughts are victorious over us—but that ends now! Stop living life based on your uncontrollable, undisciplined, ego-driven thoughts. Live instead with sustained awareness over your mind!

The most important thing we can do for our minds is to be conscious of our thoughts. Sam Harris, author of *Waking Up*, said, "The problem is not thoughts themselves but the state of thinking without being fully aware of what we are thinking." It's okay to have thoughts, but the issue occurs when we have thoughts that we have no control over. When we develop this awareness to be conscious over our thoughts, we can then replenish our mind with proper thoughts by replacing the old ones.

The last point I wish to leave you with is this: your thoughts never leave you. You can travel anywhere in the world, but those thoughts that you consistently allow into your mind out of habit—whether out of frustration, boredom, or even ego—will always be with you. You cannot escape the habit in which you think. In order to make our mind a more beautiful place so that we can live with ourselves, we desperately need to have awareness over our mind and remove and plant better thoughts. If we have control over thoughts, it doesn't matter what we do, where we are, or what we have. If our thinking controls how we feel and act, and if we can have control over our thinking, then above all we would be happy. This is the power of mastering your thoughts so that you can make your mind a beautiful place to live in no matter the circumstances.

CHAPTER 3

Clarity

A few times in my life I've had moments of clarity where the
silence drowns out the noise and I can feel rather than think.
—Tom Ford

Meditation on breathing is one of the most widely practiced Buddhist meditation techniques. It was devised and developed by the Buddha himself and he taught it during his lifetime. For 2,500 years it has been commonly studied both by monks and laypeople. During our time together, Ajahn taught me a meditation based on breath that simply focuses on one's breath and allows people to live in a state of clarity. Ajahn explained that our breath is always with us. Although it is portable and free, it is also overlooked. Many of us look toward people and pills to better ourselves when we have this gift within us that can eliminate many of the problems related to anxiety, stress, depression, etc. The notion of simply focusing and feeling your breath in and out of your nose can eliminate hindrances. This single meditation changed my mind, which caused a paradigm shift in my life and allowed me to start living my daily life in a state of clarity. Though it might *seem* easy to simply feel your breath, it is in fact the furthest thing from easy.

Ajahn stated that in our current and historical punishment system, we make the worst criminals—whether they be thieves, rapists, or even murderers—sit alone in an empty room with themselves and their breath (solitary confinement). This is the worst type of punishment according to Ajahn because all you are left with is yourself: only your thoughts and your breath. Many people would and do drive themselves mad in this setting. Any person who didn't have control over their mind would do the same. Now, he said, when we're doing this meditation, we are following the same routine as those prisoners. Even though we have a different reason for being in this setting, we're still putting ourselves in a situation akin to the one used to break down the world's most dangerous people. If we are doing what serves as the world's worst punishment, we truly should not think for a second it will be easy. However, if you are still interested in knowing the meditation that changed my life and changed the lives of many monks and people throughout history, then continue to read.

First, for this meditation to work and for you to actually experience the beauty behind it, you need to pick a duration of time in which you can do this meditation every day; as with everything in life, you have to do it consistently and with intent to actually gain the intended benefits. Therefore, before you start, honestly pick a duration of time when you know you can consistently do the meditation. The length of time it takes to do the actual meditation is determined by the actual time you have available. However, I would say that the best time for a formal meditation practice is first thing in the morning after a good night's rest. This is when the mind is most refreshed and relaxed, and it is before you start your day. The reason for doing the practice before you begin your day is that the meditation sets the tone for your entire day and gives you the opportunity to practice what you learned in your meditation in real-life experiences and situations.

When meditating, we follow the the seven-point meditation posture of legs, arms, back, eyes, jaw and mouth, tongue, and head.

1. Legs

"If possible, sit with your legs crossed in the vajra, or full lotus, position. In this position, each foot is placed, sole upward, on the thigh of the opposite leg. This position is difficult to achieve, but one can train the body to do so over time. This position gives the best support to the body and mind. However, it is not essential.

An alternative position is the half-lotus position where one foot is on the floor under the opposite leg and the other foot is on top of the opposite thigh.

A third alternative is simply sitting in a cross-legged position with both feet resting on the floor under the opposite thigh.

Sitting on a firm cushion that raises the buttocks higher than the knees can help greatly to keep the spine straight. It can also help you to sit for longer periods of time without having your feet and legs fall asleep or otherwise become uncomfortable.

If sitting on a cushion on the floor is not possible, one can use a low meditation bench. It is also perfectly acceptable to meditate while sitting on a chair. The most important thing is to find a suitable position in which you are able to be comfortable."

2. Arms

"Hold your hands loosely in your lap, right hand resting in the palm of your left, palms upward, thumbs lightly touching and forming the shape of a teardrop or flame. Your hands should be resting about 2–3

inches below the navel. Your shoulders and arms should be relaxed. Arms should be slightly akimbo, leaving a bit of space between your arms and your body to allow air to circulate. This helps to prevent sleepiness during meditation. During this seated meditation, have your hands together and thumbs touching because our mind and hands have a connection that will help with concentration."

3. Back

"Your back is most important. It should be straight and held relaxed and lightly upright, as if the vertebrae are a stack of blocks effortlessly resting in a pile. This helps your energy to flow freely and contributes greatly to the clarity and alertness of your mind in meditation. This is because our spine and back are connected. When you are reclined on your sofa watching TV, your mind is dull because your spinal cord is in a relaxed position. Therefore, when your posture is dull so too is your mind. When this is happening, you are not alert; you are relaxed. You cannot meditate like this. During your meditation your spine should be erect, which will also allow your mind to be sharp and focused. The position of your legs can contribute greatly to how easy it is to maintain a straight back; often, the higher the cushion under your buttocks and the lower your knees, the easier it is to keep a straight back. You should experiment to see what works for you."

4. Eyes

"In the beginning, it is often easier to concentrate with your eyes fully closed. This is totally fine. As you gain some experience with meditation, it is recommended that you learn to leave your eyes slightly open to let in a little light and direct your gaze downward without focusing on anything in particular. Closing the eyes completely may create a tendency toward sluggishness, sleep, or daydreaming, all of which are obstacles to clear meditation."

5. Jaw and Mouth

"Your jaw and mouth should be relaxed with your teeth slightly apart, not clenched, your lips lightly touching."

6. Tongue

"Your tongue should rest lightly on your upper palate, with the tip lightly touching the back of the upper teeth. This reduces the flow of saliva and the need to swallow. These automatic bodily actions can be hindrances to deepening your concentration, as they can become distractions."

7. Head

"Your head should be just slightly inclined forward so that your gaze is directly and naturally toward the floor in front of you. If your chin is held too high, you may have problems with mental wandering and distraction. If you drop your head too far forward, this can cause mental dullness or sleepiness."

When you are in this eyes-open position, imagine stepping into your prefrontal cortex. Ajahn explained that the prefrontal cortex is where our thoughts are generated. It is where we remember past memories, where we plan future expectations, and where our mind plans and organizes. This all happens right at the front of the forehead. Ajahn recommends we move past this during meditation by imagining there is a door that connects your prefrontal cortex to the back of your head. He said moving through the door of your busy prefrontal cortex and stepping into the back of your mind is how we discover where emptiness and clarity lie. When you move into the back of your mind, you will be at peace and the gatekeeper to each and every thought that transpires in your mind. Now your job is simple: close your eyes and breathe naturally in and out through your nose. I say "naturally" here because you don't want to force yourself to breathe every second. Instead, take a breath when you naturally have to do so. The time between breaths, keep your mind at peace and aware.

During your first meditation experiences, you may notice your mind running rapidly with thoughts. That is okay. As a matter of fact, it is great; if you are noticing these thoughts, it means you are being aware of your mind. Your mind is conditioned to always be moving forward—it is always doing its job of constantly thinking. During the breath meditation, your mind is still going to be constantly processing new thoughts, ideas, and scenarios. When you are having these thoughts, don't allow your attention to follow them; instead, just focus your attention on your breath. Ajahn explained: "The breath is observed through contact. It is not a visual, it is felt." You feel your breath by putting your attention on the beginning, middle, and end of your breath. When you simply feel your breath during the meditation, you are not stressed, worried, or thinking about the past or future. You are not planning your days or being upset. You are simply at peace, relaxed, and unbothered because you are not focusing on the part of your mind that creates all the tension and uneasiness.

During my experience with the meditation, my mind wandered to meaningless things. Ajahn taught that our minds are very tricky and will push thoughts that it knows will get your attention. Your mind is also very smart in the sense that it wants to keep you distracted from feeling clarity, because it is hardwired to always be thinking.

Your mind knows you best, so it will pick and choose thoughts to get your attention. Your mind will try everything under the sun to get your attention. Your mind has no shame, it is nasty, and it will even resort to bringing up hurtful past thoughts and experiences. Don't get outsmarted by your mind when this happens, even if the thoughts seem true or hard to ignore. Simply focus back on your breath when your mind is being restless. If you have the awareness to recognize your mind wandering, you then can refocus your attention back on your breath. Be proud when you do this because it is in itself a success. Simply noticing your mind wandering off to the past, future, stress, worry, anxiety, or even ego, and then calmly bringing that attention back is a success that we can build on. Anytime your mind tries to wander, do not get mad at yourself simply by saying to yourself, as a thought, *Back to breath.*

My mind knows that lustful thoughts will get my attention because I had a habit of always having them. Your mind will do the same with the thoughts that will get your attention, whether these are fearful, lustful, or angry. Whenever you have a thought during this meditation, use the gardening method we learned in the previous chapter to pluck your thoughts. Every time a thought comes into your mind, use the prevention method first. When you have a thought, do not engage with it; simply continue to feel your breath. If those thoughts keep coming back as repetitive thoughts, use the removal and planting method to regain your consciousness.

The last thing my mind did to try and get my attention was to attempt to convince me that I was tired during my mediation. At times, I almost feel asleep. However, you should not allow your mind to get the best of you and try to get you to sleep during this meditation. Ajahn said that, "One should not be overly rigid and excessively zealous, because this produces agitation. Neither should you be drifting into sleep from being too relaxed." This exercise should not produce excess tension or a hypnotic effect. It is an attempt to increase alertness and awareness and the capacity to sustain attention. If you succeed, you will feel a great sense of clarity, presence, and a lack of distraction. You will not feel in the least bit bored, agitated, irritated, nor will you feel in doubt. You need the middle ground, a balance between tension and drifting away. You need to find the middle ground of being relaxed yet alert.

After doing the breath meditation for the very first time at the monastery, I remember feeling a great deal of peace, calmness, and lightness in my mind and body. Right after the meditation, we took a walk outside. Once I got outside, I took a few steps on the unpaved dirt road until my eyes spotted a tree. This tree was motionless, tall, with rough edges of ingrained bark. I started to stare at the tree and continued to do so for quite some time. During this moment, I felt extremely calm, present, and happy. I didn't know this at the time but looking back on it, the reason I was so calm, present, and happy was simply because I was in a state of clarity. I realized after that being in a state of clarity is when you see things for what they truly are, without having your thoughts or emotions at the time influence what you see. The reason why I was in a clarity state was because I got into the habit of focusing on my breath which allowed me to tether myself to the actual moment I was in.

Continuously grounding your mind back to your breath helps you to see moments for what they truly are. When you breathe in and out through your nose, you pull away from your thoughts and emotions at the time and allow yourself to simply be in the moment you are in with calmness and peace on your mind. When this takes place, you feel as if you are seeing your moment in an entirely different perspective. For instance, if you take a walk down your street and have constant thoughts about the fight that took place prior with your spouse, you will see that moment in a negative light. However, take the same walk and continuously feel your breath in and out of your nose, and I promise you that you will see that modest moment of simply walking down the street in an entirely different light. This shift in your perspective of your moments takes place because when you feel your breath, your focus is on that breath alone—and not on your thoughts. That breath is present as the reality of the moment you are in. Once you feel that breath, you become tied down to reality and to the present moment. When you are in this position, you are living as your awake self and seeing your moments without the hindrances of your thoughts and emotions.

In order to continuously live in this clarity state, you need to get into the habit of practicing grounding your mind back to your breath every chance you get, so you can always be in control of how you live. Take that breath and feel it going into your nose and out again. Do this before you eat, read, step into your workplace, when you are walking to your car, driving, or even before you sleep. Do it when you're washing the dishes or hanging out with your loved ones. Be in a state of clarity wherever you go. Whether that is at the gym, work, grocery store, while reading, being at home, or hanging out with your family. You know you are in a state of clarity when your mind is not lost in thought. The amazing part of this breath is that it always gives you the opportunity to continuously live as your awake self. Every time you do not feel as if you are in a clarity state, simply take a breath in and out of your nose and truly feel that breath. There are many times throughout the day when I do not feel as peaceful as I want to, so I simply leave the moment I am in to take a breath so that I can become grounded. That two-minute break allows me to get back into my clarity state. Do this even when you are in public settings: step away and take a breath in and out through your nose to regain consciousness. That breath will allow you to wake up from living based on your habits and thoughts and will allow you to live based on who you want to be—as your conscious self. I thought I was doing too much when I did these constant check-ins, but Ajahn ensured me that these little check-ins are absolutely necessary. He told me that it is a must to check in with yourself throughout the day by focusing your attention on your breath. The more times you do this throughout the day, the more moments you live with clarity, he said. The more moments you live in clarity, the more moments you live as yourself. Many people go hours, days, weeks, and even months without taking a breath. These people live with no clarity and instead with only their unconscious habits and thoughts. For instance, did you ever say something rude to someone and quickly apologize by saying: "I am so sorry, that wasn't me. I have no idea how that came out of my mouth." For that split second in which we say those harsh words, we are not acting based on who we are but rather on the thoughts that consume our minds at that time. This leads to us acting based on how our thoughts made us feel. Imagine your mind as a helium-filled balloon. How you prevent this balloon from drifting is by tying it to your wrist. How you prevent your mind from creating stress, anger, and anxiety is by simply tying your mind to your breath; that way, your mind is grounded to reality. Allow yourself to simply be free of anger, lust, stress, worry, anxiety, and insecurities. Your mind is being held captive by your thoughts. Free yourself from this prison by relinquishing the power you gave your thoughts and simply focus on your breath by reminding yourself to do so throughout the day so that you can always practice the habit of being yourself.

In Buddhist practice, the objective is to bring what you have learned within the meditation into reality. The formal way to do the meditation is how I described it in this section. However, to practice what you learned you can use real-life activities as an opportunity to meditate on the breath. You can feel your breath while you are cleaning, going for a walk, washing dishes, and so on. By doing the clarity meditation and developing awareness over your mind by using the meditation in real-life examples, you will gradually turn into a conscious being. You develop this awareness by constantly reminding yourself to focus back on breath during the meditation. Pay attention to the moment you are in. When you do this, your thoughts are not on controlling the moment; you are instead seeing this moment for what it is by anchoring your mind to the experience. This is clarity. Live by it, because it will make your life worth living! No matter what moment you are in, anchor your mind to that moment; that moment is the only moment we have. We need to start paying attention to the moment we are in, so we may experience the fullness of clarity in that moment. For instance, when you're driving to work, practice your clarity by focusing your attention on this experience. Notice the cars on the road, the beauty of the mountains, and how you feel in this moment. When you do this, you are not thinking of anything but the moment you are in because your mind is anchored to the experience at hand. When this takes place you are calm, at peace, and present. When you go into a grocery store, instead of losing yourself in future thoughts, practice being in the moment by being mindful of your feet hitting the ground, the smell in the store, and of wishing happiness for the people around you at the time. We allow our thoughts to strip us from experiencing the fullness of the moment we are in. We walk down the street and fill our minds with constant thoughts. We go to the bank and think about the bills, the debt, the late payments. We go watch our kid's soccer game and are thinking about dinner plans. The mind is restless; it is desperate for distraction; it is always processing new ideas, sensations, scenarios, and thoughts, which means we're never in a state of clarity. Don't live another moment of your life like this. Anchor your mind to any and every experience, even if it is as simple as waiting in a bank line or walking down the street.

I asked myself the question, *how should people live every day of their existence*, and I came to the realization that people should wake up each and every day of their lives feeling in control of themselves. Never should they feel like they have no control over who they are being. They should always determine how their day is going to go by determining how they will present themselves through their thoughts, actions, reactions, and speech. Clarity is the ability to be yourself and to define yourself without being affected by any external sources or factors. Living with clarity prevents you from living a life based on your automatic habits, thoughts, and reactions. Being in a state of clarity allows you to wake up and stop living in the realm of unconsciousness. This is how people should live every day—with control over who they are, how they think, and how they act and react. They should live as conscious beings.

We suffer when we are not ourselves, and when we allow ourselves to be changed by our thoughts, other people, and external situations. We suffer when we live in our mind, continually creating scenarios and living in the past or future and never in the present. We suffer when we feel overwhelmed by our thinking by constantly focusing on any and every thought that surfaces. When you get into the habit of constantly grounding your mind back to your breath you will live in a clarity state. Living in clarity is a conscious habit that is only developed through discipline and awareness. When you take those breaths throughout your day, you are putting yourself in a state of clarity. When you are in this state, you create nirvana. Nirvana is unshakable peace. Nirvana is when you are unbothered, calm, and relaxed. Nirvana is the highest blessing of not allowing anything or anyone to affect who you are and who you want to be. When you are in nirvana, you are like the wind—nothing can move or disrupt you. When you get into the habit of grounding your mind back to your breath, it allows you to wake up from your thoughts and habits and live freely as yourself. No longer will you feel overwhelmed by your thinking. No longer will you act as a different person throughout the day by expressing anger, sadness, fear, or unhappiness. You will, quite simply, be yourself. As yourself, you will be able to live with happiness instead of with the constant suffering caused by your thoughts. You will be able to enjoy your work life, hanging out with yourself, and spending time with your family, because now you have learned how powerful your breath truly is. This simple breath and the simple instruction of telling yourself to feel that breath will allow you to live in peace and harmony, even if what is in front of you is chaotic. This breath will allow you to escape the ego-driven thoughts that run rampant through the negative space we call our mind, so we may actually see our life, our moments, and our experiences for what they are and without permitting our uncontrollable thoughts and emotions to paint the picture for us. When you use your breath as an anchor to weigh yourself down to the moment you are in, you will experience being present and you know you are present when your mind is not lost in thought. When you have a focus point that ties you down to the moment you are in, you move away from your thoughts, emotions, experiences, assumptions, judgements, and ideas, and are left with stillness, peace, and freedom. This is how you should be living every day, because this is exactly what present-moment reality is.

How to do the meditation:

- Get yourself into your position
- Set the timer
- Move away from your prefrontal cortex
- Start to breathe in and out of your nose and feel your breath
- Every time your mind wanders, simply have the thought, *back to breath*; feel pleased when you do this because this awareness is what we are striving for
- For any repetitive thought, use the gardening method of prevention by first removing, then planting
- Do this until the timer sounds

CHAPTER 4

Loving Kindness

The two basic qualities every human being

should have are love and kindness.

—Bobby Basran

Before I went to the monastery, I lived how many of you might be living right now; that is, living outside a state of loving kindness. Throughout my day, I constantly judged people based on their goals, what they ate, how they looked, how they spoke, what they drove, and what they did in life. I would only be nice and show kindness, love, and respect to those who I knew were "good" people. To the other people who I viewed as "bad," I would hope karma would find them and they would suffer for the things they had done. Anytime I heard about someone else's success, I would not wish them well; I would instead hope it wouldn't last long or would go away, because I was insecure about my own ability to achieve success. I was scared that those people would consume all of the world's success and leave me with none. This was as a result of my ego causing me to never want people to achieve glory or happiness because I truly thought they were taking it away from me. I couldn't see people being happy; my ego simply wouldn't allow it. I would think, *how can they be happy? They don't work as hard as me to find happiness; I deserve happiness more than them.*

The reason for my suffering is related to the famous Dr. Wayne Dyer example of an orange being squeezed.

Here is an excerpt from one of his seminars explaining this:

"If I were to squeeze this orange as hard as I could, what would come out?" I asked him.

He looked at me like I was a little crazy and said, "Juice, of course."

"Do you think apple juice could come out of it?"

"No!" he laughed.

"What about grapefruit juice?"

"No!"

"What would come out of it?"

"Orange juice, of course."

"Why? Why when you squeeze an orange does orange juice come out?"

He may have been getting a little exasperated with me at this point. "Well, it's an orange and that's what's inside."

I nodded. "Let's assume that this orange isn't an orange, but it's you. And someone squeezes you, puts pressure on you, says something you don't like, offends you. And out of you comes anger, hatred, bitterness, fear. Why? The answer, as our young friend has told us, is because that's what's inside."

Whatever is inside you is the very thing that will come out of you. In my situation, if you squeezed me, what would have come out would be anger, envy, judgement, frustration, and negativity. It is impossible to live a life filled with happiness, peace, and joy when the very thing inside you is the exact opposite. Therefore, I had to change what was inside me to start living a more happy, peaceful, and joyful external life—and what allowed me to do so was a simple meditation practice that I learned during my time at the monastery that was called loving kindness meditation.

A loving kindness meditation is a practice in which you wish wellness, happiness, and peace for all beings through your level of thinking. You start by getting into your meditative position, whether that is in a chair or being seated. You then set a timer for 5-20 minutes depending on how much time you have and your experience with meditation. After that, you breathe in and out through your nose to ground yourself to the moment you are in. Once you are grounded to the present moment, you begin to wish wellness, happiness, and peace for all beings. You start by wishing people who you love dearly (parent, sibling, or child) wellness, happiness, and peace. When the person you are wishing wellness, happiness, and peace comes into your mind, truly take your time and think to yourself, *what do I want to wish for this person? What does live well for this person mean? What would make this person truly happy? How would this person be truly at peace with their life?* Each person you are wishing goodwill for will have a different view of wellness, happiness, and peace. This means you truly have to think of each individual with great intent while doing this practice.

Here is an example of my loving kindness meditation:

I want to wish goodwill through loving kindness to Sunny. I hope he is well and he lives a long, healthy, and beautiful life with no diseases or illnesses. I hope he is happy and gets all the success that he has ever dreamt about. I hope he gets the fame, money, success, houses, cars, and everything in between. I hope his business is a massive success and he is a worldwide fashion icon. I hope he has a beautiful, healthy family. I hope he is at peace with the life he chooses to create.

I want to wish goodwill through loving kindness to Anita. I hope she is well, and she lives a long, healthy, and beautiful life with no diseases or illnesses. I hope she is happy, finds her purpose in life, and has massive amounts of success from doing so. Whether that comes from opening her own vegan restaurant or becoming a designer. And I hope she uses her success to take care of her family. I hope she is at peace, knowing her mum is in a better place and has a beautiful relationship with her sister. I hope she is at peace with her life and happy with the life we have created together where we both do our purpose, have amazing and healthy kids, travel the world, and live at peace in our big beautiful home.

I want to wish goodwill through loving kindness for Journey. I hope she is well and lives a long, healthy, and beautiful life with no diseases or illnesses. I hope she is happy and wakes in the morning as the happiest person alive and goes to bed with a smile on her face. During the day, I hope she gets to play with the people she loves to be around: her mom, dad, uncles, aunts, grandmas, and grandpas. I hope she is at peace with her life and never suffers a day in her precious life.

I want to wish goodwill through loving kindness for Owen. I hope is well and lives a long, healthy, and beautiful life. I hope he is happy and never suffers. I hope he gets to eat great food, does the things he loves every day, and gets to spend time with the people who care for him. I hope he is at peace with his life and spends his days with his mom, brother, and grandpa as a beautiful healthy family.

This is just my understanding of what wellness, happiness, and peace means to me; yours might be completely different. Similarities and differences don't matter; as long as you are wishing well for all the people who come to your mind, you are on the right path to living a life in a state of loving kindness. These are just four people of fifteen to twenty people I wish wellness, happiness, and peace for.

It is easy to wish all this goodness for people who you love dearly, who are good to you, and who have done no wrong—but this is not the entire meditation. Ajahn stated that we should wish loving kindness for all beings, even those who may have done you wrong in the past or wrong in general. He explained that it might be hard to wish good for people who have done a lot of terrible things to you, so we should start off small by wishing wellness, happiness, and peace for someone who we really adore, and work our way up from there. Eventually, you want to develop the frame of mind in which you wish loving kindness for all beings, no matter who they are or what they have done; doing so means you are always filled with loving kindness.

Imagine that every day you practice wishing loving kindness for people in this manner. Think of how joyful your life would be when you practice wishing loving kindness for someone other than yourself. Every single time I do this meditation, I am left with pure happiness and bliss running through my body, a smile on my face, and peace on my mind. The reason we should want to do this meditation every single day is to develop the habit of wishing loving kindness for all people without requirements and conditions. When we consistently do this meditation, we move closer to living in a love and kindness state. When I interviewed Ajahn, he told me he has been practicing this exact loving kindness meditation for the past thirty years. He told me there is no better state to live in, and I couldn't agree more. To me, loving kindness is a state of being one should always live in. Loving kindness is when you understand people rather than judge them. Loving kindness is wishing no harm or suffering to anyone, no matter who they are or what they have done to you or to other people. Loving kindness is wishing happiness, success, and peace for all individuals, including yourself. Loving kindness is when you see the good in everything, whether that be people, places, situations, experiences, or moments. Loving kindness is when you are simply kind and respectful to yourself and all other beings. Loving kindness is when you remove your ego entirely and are free from anger by wishing happiness for others. When you are in this state, you don't cause any anger or suffering toward yourself or others, whether this is through your thoughts, words, actions, or reactions. You are simply an aura of positive energy.

The first thing that being in a loving kindness state does is remove our ego. Our ego is self-centered and only cares about one person. However, when we are in a loving kindness state, we practice wishing well for all people, which allows us to kill our ego on the spot. When we have no ego, we will start to live a happier life. For example, if I'm not in a loving kindness state and someone gives me advice, my ego will think this person is trying to criticize me or thinks they're better than me or that I'm better than the person giving me the advice, so I don't need their advice. However, if I was in a loving kindness state of being, I would think how amazing it is that this person is taking time out of their day to help me. The difference between these two responses is created by the state of being we want to live our lives in.

Another example of ego is how we are negative when we hear about someone's success. This is because as human beings we typically have an ego. Your ego causes blockages that do not allow you to be happy for someone else's success.

50

Your ego says, *how come they got their success? I deserve it.* Your ego doesn't want people to do well because that's a sign that they are growing closer to their goals; your ego only wants you, and no one else, to get there. We become resentful of someone else's possessions, qualities, faith, and success. How many times throughout your day do you hear about someone's success and fail to express loving kindness and instead become jealous? At this very moment, think about the thoughts you are having. Your thoughts of jealousy and hatred are not going to slow down the other person's success and are not going speed up yours—all they are doing is allowing you to live without happiness and peace. However, when you wish loving kindness towards people, you teach yourself to truly wish the very best for people, which allows you to be more loving and caring and less egotistical.

Second, being in a state of loving kindness allows you to always see the good in your moments. When I started to live in a state of loving kindness, what was inside was projecting out into the world, and what was inside me was happiness, peace, and joy. No matter what I was doing, I would see the good in it. I believe this is because when you are in loving kindness, you do not have negative thoughts weighing you down, which in turn allows you to reframe your situation more positively. For instance, before you read, if you have thoughts regarding how reading is a chore, how it is dull, and how you hate sitting still, then your experience of reading will be negative. However, if before you read you have thoughts of how this is going to be an amazing experience and you have the ability to learn and grow from this time, your experience of reading will be quite positive. The two experiences of reading stay the same, and the only thing that changes is your thoughts related to the experience. Therefore, your experiences are created by your thoughts. If you change your thoughts, you change the basis of your experiences. When we are in a loving kindness state, we are not bogged down by our negative thoughts and instead see the good in our moments instead of the bad.

Third, being in a state of loving kindness allows you to always understand people rather than judge them. This is largely due to the fact that when you're in a state of loving kindness your ego is entirely removed, which allows you to develop empathy for people. This feeling of empathy would not be possible if you had an ego, since the ego is self-centered.

You understand that hurt people, hurt people. You understand that everyone is different, and that people have different perspectives. You understand that people grow up in different environments and conditions that mold them into the people they are today. With this newfound perspective of always understanding rather than judging, you move away from reacting with anger and frustration to simply being your loving and kind self.

For example, one day my girlfriend was being quite rude to me. Her speaking without a purpose and using hateful words caused an unpleasant end to our evening. When she was about to walk me to the front door, I looked at her and gave her a hug and said, "I know your hurt, and I am not going to react because I understand that hurt people, hurt people." Instead of fighting back and making the matter worse I took a minute to realize that this was happening because of a bigger issue. A few days later, she told her sister the same story and said that me understanding rather than judging her was helpful because it made her realize she was speaking through her emotions at the time. The reason I share this story with you is to suggest that people should always seek to understand other people and situations because when you do, you never react in a negative manner; you simply remain your loving and kind self, because you seek to understand rather than judge.

The last thing that being in a loving kindness state does is help us wish well for all people no matter who they are or what they have done. Everyone on the face of the planet is worthy of loving kindness. When you have this type of mindset, you no longer suffer. Think of how many times you are negative throughout the day by wishing badly for people, judging them, or being rude to them. Think about your boss saying something that you do not agree with; what do you do? Do you have angry thoughts about her? Your family member says something that irritates you; what do you do? Do you have aggressive thoughts about them? You see the person who has done so much wrong to you; what do you do? Do you stew in your anger of how much you hate that person? I find it ironic that many people allow the mere presence of someone or the mention of their name to cause themselves to suffer by being filled with negativity and rage. Why are you going to not allow yourself to live happily, at peace, and joyfully every day? Who is so important that they have the power to determine how you should be living? It doesn't matter what people say or do to you; you should always wish them loving kindness. Harboring negativity toward people or situations, no matter the severity of what either has done to you or to others, will not allow you to be truly happy. However, when you are in a loving kindness state, no single person or thing can take away your happiness. For example, if a family member says a rude or condescending comment to you and you wish badly for them, have negative thoughts about them, or react with anger, you are actually stripping yourself of your own happiness. I used to do the same thing. I would see people who didn't have big goals and would judge them. I couldn't be happy in these moments, because I was so filled with judgement. People would say rude things to me, and I gave them the power to control me by my stewing in my own angry thoughts.

One individual who motivates me to always be in loving kindness is Dr. Martin Luther King Jr. No matter what was thrown his way, Dr. King never acted out of the character God called him to be in. He went through so much and yet never gave people the satisfaction of allowing their actions to cause him suffering. Dr. King's house got bombed on multiple occasions, people would retaliate against his loving kindness with physical and verbal violence, people would humiliate him, but through it all he was calm and collected and stayed within his character. One example that changed my view of always being in loving kindness is when Dr. King was preaching and a person joined him on stage. Dr. King thought the person was just coming up to say something, but the person actually took a swing at him. Dr. King fell to the ground and by then people had come to his rescue and pulled the man off him. While still trying to recover from the blow to his face, Dr. King yelled, "Don't hit him, he needs us to pray for him." Read that example and look at your own life. How many times a day do you find yourself suffering because of what someone said or did to you? How many times do you suffer in your own mind when you wish badly for people, have an ego toward people, or wish for karma to find people?

In the Buddha scripture it once said, "When people speak badly of you, you should respond in this way: keep a steady heart and don't reply with harsh words. Practice letting go of resentment and accepting that the other's hostility is the spur to your understanding. Be kind, adopt a generous standpoint, treat your enemy as a friend, and suffuse all your world with affectionate thoughts, far reaching and widespread, limitless and free from hate. In this state you should try to remain." There is always going to be someone who causes suffering to others. But don't give them more satisfaction by continually allowing them to cause your suffering.

You are allowing people and situations to cause you suffering, but you may read that statement and ask, "But what if the person I am wishing hatred for is a horrible person? What if this person did something wrong to me? What if this person tried to sleep with my girlfriend? What if this person committed rape? What if this person killed someone? What if this person is a gut-wrenchingly horrible person who lives only to cause my suffering?" Always remember that it is never about who the person is or what they have done to you or in general; it is about who *you* are, who you want to be, and how you want to live. Why allow a person or situation to cause you even more suffering? What are your angry, resentful, and frustrated thoughts going to achieve? Are they going to fix what has already taken place? No. Are they going to make the pain hurt less? No. All that is going to come from you filling yourself with anger and negativity is that you strip yourself of your happiness, peace, and joy. However, if you are in a loving kindness state and wish well for all people and situations without conditions, you will not suffer at the hands of your own mind. We suffer when we are anything but happy and at peace throughout our day. Life is way too short to spend in a negative state, even if it is for an hour a day or a couple of days a week. Think about the people and situations that cause you so much suffering and now wish those things loving kindness and watch yourself transcend into happiness.

People suffer daily by being negative, angry, and depressed, and by filling ourselves with nothing but those things. We hear someone's name or what a person has done, and right away we are drowned in a sinkhole of negativity. Why? Why give someone the power to change who we are? We should value our happiness and well-being more than that. I found that when you wish loving kindness for all people, they no longer have the ability to change who you are—and I am not the only person with this mindset.

Anthony Ray Hinton was wrongfully accused and sent to jail for thirty years for a crime he did not commit. Finally, after he nearly spent half of his life in a cell, he was released. During his interview on *60 Minutes*, correspondent Scott Pelley asked Mr. Hinton if he was angry after the State of Alabama took three decades of his life. Mr. Hinton said he was not angry. "They took 30 years of my life, as you said. What joy I have I cannot afford to give that to them." Being angry, he said, would be "letting them win." Mr. Hinton explained, "I am a person that loves to laugh. I love to see other people smile. And how can I smile when I'm full of hate?" Having anger within us toward people and situations robs us of the ability to experience happiness. Read the previous example and understand that when you harbor anger, judgement, and frustration within yourself toward any person no matter what they have done, you will continue to suffer.

The only way to move past this is by wishing loving kindness for all beings without conditions.

Every time I do this meditation, I cannot help but smile and feel radiant with happiness when I wish loving kindness for my family, friends, and those people who don't see life the same way I do—I would say enemies here, however I do not have any because, as a result of this meditation, I wish well for all people. Imagine how beautiful, peaceful, and happy your life would be if you practiced the habit of wishing loving kindness for all people, even your worst enemies, even the people who make the hair stand up on the back of your neck, even the people who you think were put on this earth to cause you suffering. You have to understand that the more you allow yourself to hold anger and frustration within yourself toward any person or situation, the more you are causing yourself to suffer. Think back to the Dr. Wayne Dyer example of squeezing the orange. Whatever is inside you will come out if enough pressure is exerted upon you. If anger, ego, and frustration is constantly inside you, when life happens and someone says something rude, then what is inside you will be projected into the universe. You have to understand that it is never about who the person is or what they have done; it is about who you are, who you want to be, and how you want to live your life. Why are you allowing a person to force you to live in a realm of frustration, anger, and hatred, when all you have to do is wish well for them and free yourself from the chains of suffering? Do this meditation every day and you will restore your immediate happiness and also create long-lasting happiness. Just imagine that every single day you block out time to wish loving kindness for ten, fifteen, twenty, twenty-five, thirty people. Eventually this meditation will transcend your everyday life and you will unconsciously begin to wish loving kindness for people. When this happens, you will begin to live in a state of loving kindness. Continue to live in this state by constantly asking yourself daily, *what state of being am I in?* This will trigger you to jump back into the state of loving kindness if you are not already in it.

What causes us to suffer immensely in the first place is our reactions to people and situations. However, when we are living in a state of loving kindness, we remove our ego, see the good in every situation and wish people unconditional love. When we harness this power of loving kindness, we have no hate, frustration or anger inside of us. Therefore, when life's hands start to grip us tightly by sending people and situations our way to see what will come out of us, life will be surprised when all that comes out is happiness, peace and joy.

When you are at this stage in life, you will never suffer and will always have unshakable peace that allows you to live in nirvana. The biggest thing that affects us is other people. If it wasn't something they did, it was something they said that caused us to be angry, jealous, or frustrated. How many times can you count a single person saying or doing something that dictated your energy, your mood, your joy, your happiness? One too many, I presume. I promise you that once you start to live in a loving kindness state, other people will no longer hold the key to your happiness, joy, and peace. We need to harness inner peace and inner peace only begins the moment we choose not to allow another person or event to control our emotions. When we simply wish other people well through loving and kindness, we begin to live with nirvana—unshakable peace.

Chapter 5

Finding Pleasure in Your Simple Moments

If you can't find pleasure in the simple or the mundane

then you won't find pleasure anywhere.

—Mark Manson

Life is made up of simple moments: going to the grocery store, having family dinners, watching a movie with your kids, going on a date with your significant other, reading a book, working on your purpose, or simply spending time in solitude. Many of us struggle to find pleasure in these simple moments because our focus is not on the present happening right in front of us, but rather on the past or the future. When our mind isn't present in the moment we are creating, we tend to have a difficult time seeing the good in that particular moment. Just as we cannot see something without looking at it, we cannot see the good in our moment without giving our attention to that very moment.

I could not for the life of me find pleasure in my simple moments. If I tried watching a movie, my mind would worry about how my mom could die before I was able to bless her in ways I'd always dreamed about. If I tried reading a book, would instantly have thoughts of wanting to watch porn. If I was taking my niece to the park, my mind would be racing in the future of what I was going to be doing afterward. My mind was constantly searching for a distraction. When the search for distraction took place during my moments, it distanced me from seeing the good in the moment I was creating; I was not truly present. This not only affected me, but the people around me as well, because when I was not fully present in the moment, I was truly not bringing the best version of myself. However, once I read the above quote by Mark Manson, my life instantly changed. I thought to myself, *If I cannot find pleasure in the simple moments of watching a movie or hanging out with my niece, then I will suffer most of my life, because most of my life will be filled with simple moments such as these.* I understood that I needed to develop the habit of finding pleasure in my moments—no matter how simple they were.

To find pleasure in simple moments is to be in these moments without suffering in the core of your own mind. Suffering in this instance is when you aren't in a state of clarity, because when you aren't in a state of clarity you are not seeing your moments for what they truly are; you are seeing these moments based on the thoughts that are consuming in your mind. For example, you can be watching your favorite TV show, but if you're constantly dwelling on the future and thinking about what may happen in the next six months, you will not see the beauty of the moment because it is being tainted by your undisciplined mind being elsewhere. Another example is: If I placed your wife in front of you but also placed my hands in front of your eyes at the same time you would not be able to see your beautiful, loving wife standing in front of you. This is simply because your vision is blocked by an external object. No matter what I put in front of you, no matter how amazing it is, you would not be able to see it. This same principle of not seeing what is front of you because of an external object applies to how you see your life. You cannot see the beauty of your life and the experiences that are right in front of you, no matter how amazing they are if your thoughts are preventing you from seeing what is in front of you. In order to see the beauty of your life, you need to move beyond your thinking and be in a state of clarity. To do so, you must feel your breath in the moments you are in so that you can immerse yourself in that moment. When your mind is grounded to the present moment by being tied down to your breath your thoughts cannot affect what you see. This will always allow you to always see life for what it truly is – a precious gift.

People will try to say, *The moment I am in right now is horrible—nothing good is happening.* My response is simple: how you act in one moment is how you will act in all of your moments. If you find something that prevents you from enjoying the moment you are in now, then you will always find something that prevents you from enjoying the moment you are in, because in life nothing is ever perfect. Life is filled with limited moments. Because we do not know when our last one will come, we should enjoy each and every single one of them. If we wait to enjoy our moments until we have no stress and worries, we will waste our entire life waiting for something that may never come. There is no perfect moment, for anything. There is always going to be something less than ideal that arises in your life. Today, it is your tenants that cause you to find little pleasure during your coffee date with your spouse; tomorrow it is the fact that you got fired from your job that causes you to fail to enjoy any of your moments for the next six months. Don't get into the habit of allowing the problems that arise in your life to affect your moments, because life—good or bad—is always happening, and we shouldn't stop living because of it. Don't think that when you reach your purpose or have achieved financial freedom is when you can start to enjoy your moments. Just because you're rich and successful doesn't mean you are immune to life and its troubles. Problems are always going to happen—they are a part of life. Stop waiting for life to be perfect to enjoy your moments, because life is never going to be perfect, but that does not mean you cannot enjoy it.

Understand that this is your moment! Whether that moment is you accepting an award at the Grammys, going on a vacation, watching TV, or simply spending time with your loved ones. Whether that moment is sad, boring, exciting, dull, or eventful, it is your moment and you need to find peace in it. The way you do this is by being present in that moment with your breath, and by grounding your mind through your breath so that you can fully enjoy the moment by not having your mind elsewhere. When your mind is not being bogged down by your thinking, you can start to notice the beauty within that moment. Go for coffee with your loved one and when you are sitting there, just feel your breath. Only then will you see that moment for what it truly is. All of our moments are beautiful; we just never see them that way because our mind is focusing somewhere or on something else. This is an extremely important practice, always feeling your breath in the moment you are in, because again, how you live in one moment will affect how you live in all of your moments.

You can learn to be present in your moments by accepting them as a part of your life or you can pass the moment by being distracted. Just remember, how you pick to respond to your moment will turn into a habit of how you respond to all of your moments. For instance, if I didn't develop the ability to appreciate the simple moments like hanging out with my niece because I thought another moment would be better, I would be building a habit of constantly trying to find a better moment to be in. This cycle of always looking into the future for a "better" moment would never truly allow me to enjoy experiences. Appreciate the moment you are in. Life is always changing, and this moment will never return. I always remind myself of this, whether I am reading a book or watching a movie by myself. I tell myself, *be in this moment and appreciate it, because it will never come back.* If you don't practice appreciation for the moment you are in now, what makes you think you're going to appreciate the moments to come? Even if you think the moments that are yet to come are better than the current ones, what makes you think you will appreciate them? Finding pleasure in your moments is habit-based. You need to develop the habit of finding pleasure in the moments that are in your life right now, or else you will never appreciate what comes simply because you didn't practice appreciation for what you had.

We all have so many beautiful moments throughout the day, whether while driving to work, spending time watching our favorite shows, cooking with our moms, talking to our partners, or even playing with our children. Unfortunately, we just cannot see the beauty within these moments, because our thoughts don't allow us to be truly present within them. However, once we move away from our thoughts by grounding our minds to our breath, we can then find pleasure in our simple moments by being grateful for them. When you develop this perspective of being present and appreciating all of your moments, you will always find pleasure in your life. When you get to this level, you will live with nirvana—unshakable peace.

Three things to remember to help you find pleasure in your simple moments:

1. Feel your breath in the moment you are in to ground yourself so that you can see the moment for what it truly is.
2. Have the perspective to always see the good in your moments.
3. Understand the habit of how you act in your moments. How you act in one moment is how you are going to act in all of your moments.

CHAPTER 6

Having Faith

How you get so much favor on your side?
Accept him as your lord and savior I replied.

—Kanye West

For me, faith is believing that there is a higher power and that power watches over us and doesn't allow us to walk this journey we call life alone. Whether you believe that higher power is God, fate, karma, destiny, energy, or a higher spirit is your choice. But what I would like to suggest is to have faith, because when we do, we have reassurance over those things we cannot control. I want to teach people the importance of having faith through three things: 1) When you're marked, you don't have to fight battles that God has already fought for you; 2) A blessing never looks like a blessing; and; 3) Understanding your season. The reason I want to teach people to have faith through these three things is to ensure they stop living their daily lives with stress, worry, fear, and anxiety, and start to live their daily lives with peace, happiness, and joy. The best way I found to live in this nirvana state is by having faith.

When you're marked, you don't have to fight battles that God has already fought for you.

I worked at a company for years that I loved. I never had any issues or problems with any of my colleagues or management. I was a great employee and did my job well. However, one day I got a new manager, and this was to be the first time I had a work problem. This new manager was a dictator who wanted things done her way; she abused her power and made people feel small and scared. During the time when this person managed me, she told other people false stories about me that ended up painting a negative picture of me. She tried making an example out of me by using her power and title. At work, I felt like I had no one and that the whole company was against me, as they didn't do anything to help me. I phoned HR, who made it seem like it wasn't a big deal. For weeks, I was scared; it took a huge toll on me. Throughout my day I would be filled with so much worry, fear, and stress that it started to affect my life. I couldn't concentrate on anything other than this very problem, and every time I tried to focus, my mind would remind me again. *What if this person tells untrue stories about me and I lose my job? How am I going to make ends meet? What will I do for work until my purpose turns into my full-time work?* I know I am not alone in this predicament. I know many of you live as I was living, by allowing a thing, you have no control over to control you. We spend our time that is meant to be spent in happiness, peace, and joy worrying about things we cannot control, whether it is your coworker who keeps getting under your skin, your family members who always seem like they are out to get you, or what other people say or do. I had no control over how this person treated me and talked badly about me, or if I was going to lose my job over something she said about me. But during this time, I couldn't see that. All I could see was my stress, worry, and fear related to the situation and that caused me to live as if there was a constant black cloud hovering over me. I would have continued to live in this state of suffering if I didn't stumble across a pastor who helped me to start living with faith. One day at work, I watched a sermon by Michael Todd, the lead pastor at Transformation Church, and it changed my life.

The one phrase that stood out to me during this sermon was "When you're marked by God, you don't have to fight battles that God has already fought for you." This means that when you have faith in God all you have to do is not act out of the character, he called you to be in and allow what you simply cannot control to be taken care of through faith.

While dealing with my problem with my manager, I was acting out of the character God intended me to be in. I would speak badly about her; I would respond with anger whenever she texted me, and I would have horrible negative thoughts about her. But after watching the sermon, I intended to change my ways. Anytime someone mentioned her name, I would only speak good things about her. Anytime she contacted me, I made sure not to change myself—I would respond to her with loving kindness because that's the person I was and wanted to be. Any time my mind tried to bring up this problem, I would say to myself, *When you're marked by God you don't have to fight battles that God has already fought for you, all you have to do is not act out of the character he called you to be in,* and instantly my worry, stress, and fear would dissipate and I started to live in happiness, joy, and peace. The very problem that was controlling me no longer had control over me. I just had faith in God that if I truly didn't act out of the character he called me to be in, he would take care of it. A few weeks passed and I received an email from my HR manager asking if I could come in for a meeting. Normally, I would live in complete worry and fear until the day of the meeting, but this time I just felt different, a good different. I chose not to allow something that I had no control over to affect me. I didn't live with fear, worry, or stress; I just continued to live my happy, conscious life. Turns out the meeting was to address how that manager was mistreating me. The HR team assured me this problem would stop right away. I had no further incidents with the very person who was causing me so much grief and frustration.

The reason I share this story with you is the same reason I wrote this book: I want to teach people to no longer live their limited days on this earth with fear, stress, and worry in their minds. Our reality is truly a reflection of what is in our minds, and if we continuously live with hindrances, then our reality will be no different. I want people to live their days on this earth with happiness, peace, and joy, but that is impossible if we keep living in a state of worry, fear, and stress over the things we can't control. You have no control over whether your tenants are going to vandalize your place. You have no control over how your coworker mistreats you. You have no control over whether your boss decides to fire you one day. You have no control over how your family member is being rude to you. You have no control over how people treat you. Many people don't realize this and spend their time thinking, dwelling, and creating negativity, anger, and anxiety in their minds by focusing their attention on the very things they have no control over. The next time you find yourself, through awareness, living in a state of fear, stress, or worry, remind yourself that when you're marked by God you don't have to fight battles that God has already fought for you. The very problem you are worrying about, the one that you spend all of your time thinking about, the one that causes you to live in a state of suffering has already been fixed for you. All he wants in return is for you to not act out of the character he called you to be in, and in time for you to see how powerful he truly is.

The reason why he asks you to not act out of the character he called you to be in is because the one thing you can always control is yourself, whether in the form of your thoughts, words, actions, or reactions. You can't control how your family member treats you, but you can control how you respond. You can't control if your new manager is rude, but you can control how you talk about her. That person who keeps getting under your skin and on your last nerve has already been taken care of by God, so all you need to do is not change your character in a negative manner. Remain your true self, because you are a vessel sent by God and he does not want his people to act in a way that he would never act. This means you need to show love, compassion, and kindness at a time when people are showing anger, hate, and ego. This is no easy task; I know from experience. It wasn't easy for me to show kindness to a person who was so disrespectful, hateful, and negative toward me, but I understood I had to show kindness, because I know I am a vessel sent by God and he would not want one of his pupils to act in a way that he would never act. Be the bigger person and never act out of the character God called you to be in. By doing so, through faith, God will take care of your situation.

How many times a day do we lose our happiness, peace, and joy by dwelling on a situation, outcome, or problem that we cannot control? I would find myself living in negativity because I kept worrying, stressing, and creating frustration within my mind by constantly thinking about a problem that I had no control over. I would sit and dwell about whether my tenant's paperwork would go through so I could evict them. I had no control over this decision, but I would worry about it daily. The only thing I could control was sending the paperwork off, which I did, but I would still live in fear, worry, and stress until the decision was made. *Are they going to accept my application? What if they don't? What am I going to do? Are my tenants going to burn my place down?* All these thoughts and more wouldn't allow me to live in a state of nirvana—unshakable peace. I learned that I needed to have faith to create a life filled with happiness, peace, and joy.

Our days are numbered from the minute we are born. Our time is therefore precious and limited, so do not waste your time living in a state of fear or stress by worrying about things you can't control. Through faith, understand that when you're marked by God you don't have to fight battles that he has already fought for you. Now when a problem arises in my life, I truly just smile. I control what I control—whether that includes my reaction, my attitude, my character, or my words—which allows me to not act out of the character God called me to be in, and then I say to myself with a smile on my face and faith in my heart, *When you're marked, you don't have to fight battles that God has already fought for you.*

A blessing never looks like a blessing.

One day my girlfriend and I were picking up her sister from work. She had told me beforehand that her sister might be getting fired from her job, which she had been working at for six years. When her sister got into the car and told us she got fired, I mumbled a line to myself: *"A blessing never looks like a blessing."* At the time, I truly didn't know what this meant; it just sort of came to me in the moment. Throughout the car ride home, my girlfriend and her sister kept discussing the firing. My girlfriend asked her sister if she would have ever left her comfortable job on her own, and her sister said no. Even though she knew that this job didn't serve her purpose or make her truly happy, she would never had left. The message here and throughout this section is simple: *A blessing never looks like a blessing.*

How do you know a bad moment from a good one? How do you know if getting declined by a publishing company is the end of your story and not just the beginning of it? Throughout your life when you have big disappointments, failures, and even setbacks—whether that is being fired from your job, getting rejected from an investor on your new startup, or even breaking your leg—how do you know that the particular situation is a bad moment and not a good moment? In her book *When Things Fall Apart,* Pema Chödrön offers an example of how we don't know the difference between a bad moment and a good moment. She writes: "I have a friend dying of AIDS. Before I was leaving for a trip we were talking. He said, 'I didn't want this, and I hated this, and I was terrified of this. But it turns out that this illness has been my greatest gift.' He said, 'now every moment is so precious to me. All the people in my life are so precious to me. My whole life means so much to me.' Something had really changed, and he felt ready for his death. Something that was horrifying and scary has turned into a gift."

Now I ask you, after reading that example, how do you perceive the moments in your life that you think are your "end-all" moments? These are the moments when everything seems so dark that you cannot see even a glimpse of lightness. The moments where you didn't get the promotion you wanted or when your manufacturer refuses to make your clothes. These are the moments when you tear your Achilles in the middle of your boxing career. How do you perceive these moments? I honestly believe most people interpret those moments as, *Why did this happen to me? Why is the world out to get me? Why didn't God help me? Why does everything bad happen to me?* Most people view those moments in a negative light, therefore allowing themselves to sink into a negative state. They may get fired from their job and think for days on end about what is going to happen next. Or they get rejected from a book publishing company and start to live in fear by second-guessing their purpose. They may get news about a disease and start to live in constant fear and worry, which prevents them from living their everyday life with happiness and peace. When these moments happen, remember that they are meant to tear down a regular person, so stand tall and accept them with open arms. Do not waste your precious time living in fear and worrying about those moments, because you don't know what's on the other side of them. I got rejected from getting into an education program that would have qualified me to become a teacher. When that experience took place, I had two options: Live daily with stress and fear about what was to come next and continuously ask why this happened to me or understand that this happened for a reason and something greater was in store for me. Now I am the author of a book, I have my own podcast and I live out my dreams daily. If you have a mindset of perceiving your biggest "losses" in the lens of *a blessing never looks like a blessing*, you will always move forward by constantly growing as an individual and will never bring yourself down when "bad" moments occur. Through faith, understand a blessing never looks like a blessing, because your greatest disappointment, failure, rejection, or setback could be the spark to your greatest accomplishment, success, and blessing in life.

Reed Hastings and Marc Randolph are the founders of the juggernaut streaming video-on-demand service Netflix. Today Netflix is known as one of the most historic start-ups; however, just like all successful people, Hastings and Randolph had to climb up the mountain of success and battle hardships, adversity, and failure. In the year 2000, Netflix was on track to report a loss of $50 million. During their company's financial trouble, the founders wanted to set up a meeting for months with their brick-and-mortar competition, which at the time was Blockbuster. Blockbuster's owners finally decided to meet with the young entrepreneurs. During this meeting, the Netflix owners wanted to sell their company to Blockbuster for $50 million so that they could cut their losses and be done with the company. Blockbuster's CEO and executives listened to the at-the-time "crazy" sales pitch and ultimately laughed Netflix out the door. On the plane ride home, Marc spoke to his friend and said, "Blockbuster doesn't want us, so it's obvious what we have to do now, it looks like now we're going to have to kick their ass." The reason I share this story is so that you have a real-life understanding of how a blessing never looks like a blessing. Netflix could have looked at this moment the very same way many of us view our "bad" moments in life by rolling over, questioning our own abilities and purpose, and constantly living in fear and worry. But they didn't, and neither should you—ever. I truly believe every experience we have in life, no matter how bad it seems, holds a blessing; our goal is to find it, because if we live with this perspective of always finding the blessing in all of our situations, we will forever live with peace, happiness, and joy.

Understand your season.

Understanding your season means knowing that the events that take place in your life, good or bad, happen for a reason; your job is to find that reason to prevent yourself from living with regret, depression, anger, and resentment.

To illustrate my point of understanding your season, I would like to share a story:

Damian Lillard is an NBA all-star point guard for the Portland Trail Blazers, however before he was an NBA star, he was an ambitious kid with dreams of going pro. During his high school career, he and his friends would discuss going to the NBA. His friends at the time would say they wanted to go to the NBA whereas Damian would say, "I *need* to go to the NBA." For Damian, it was a *must* and not a *want*.

During one of his high school games, a single scout showed up. In this particular game, Damian outplayed everyone on the entire court. After the game, the head coach of Weber State University, coach Randy Rahe, offered Damian a scholarship.

During his first year at Weber State, Damian received the freshman of the year award. During his sophomore year, he was the MVP of the entire league. In his junior year, his dreams of going to the NBA were turning into a reality when he saw his name on the NBA draft board. However, things took a wild and unexpected turn when Damian broke his foot the year he was about to enter the draft. This was a hard pill to swallow because Damian would've been a first-round lottery pick in this draft class, because of his amazing play the season before in college. But with his injury, he didn't even see his name on the draft board. What once seemed like an eventuality—going to the NBA—now looked like a distant dream for Damian, so he decided not to join the draft class that year, which took a mental toll on him because he thought many scouts would not want an older player as a draft prospect. Due to his injury Damian decided not to go into the draft and to return to Weber State to rehab and play one more year of college basketball.

During this *season* of his life, Damian used the time he had to his advantage. Within this period, in which most people would have questioned God and their position in life, Damian used it as an opportunity to improve skills. His trainer said during the four to six months Damian was injured, he used the time to get better at things he normally wouldn't have the time to work on. Damian's brother said he became who he is when he broke his foot. During Damian's injury his brother saw him get into a new mindset. It was the first time he saw his brother lifting weights, competing during conditioning, and actually starting to bust his ass. This added work separated Damian in the long run, his trainer said. The year after Damian's broken foot, he averaged 24.5 points per game and led the nation in scoring throughout most of the year and saw his name back on the NBA draft board. In his pre-draft combine, he had the strength and conditioning that he could only have developed through his "tough time" to outbattle his competition and earn himself to be the sixth pick in the 2012 NBA draft, followed by being named the NBA Rookie of The Year that same year.

My reason for sharing this story is to help illustrate the point that God knows exactly what you have to go through in order to be the person he destined you to be. The minute you were born, God instilled a tailor-made purpose in you, therefore he knows exactly what you have to go through in order to accept, sustain, and thrive in your destiny. Just look at Damian's story as proof. Right before he was going to live out his destiny that God created him to do, he broke his leg. This unexpected turn of events could have caused Damian to question God's motive and start to live as a victim, which most people end up doing when a setback happens by living with self-pity, repressed anger, and a poor outlook. However, if you have the perspective of understanding your season by knowing God has created your destiny, you are able to look back on your tough times and understand that God only puts you in those times of difficulty so that you can be ready for what he has called you to be. Damian's own brother told him, "God didn't think you were ready, so he broke your leg." And he was absolutely right, because Damian became the player he is today thanks to that time of triumph. In Damian's situation, God was giving him a setback so that when he got to his destiny, he would be able to accept it, sustain it, and thrive in it.

What you have been through or going through is not a surprise to God, because God has written every page in your book. Therefore, God has you in the very place you are in right now not to take you out, but to build the person he destined you to be. You may not see it from this perspective yet, since the place you are in may seem very challenging to overcome, but just know that this doesn't mean you're not meant to be in the position you are in right now, no matter how difficult it may look or seem; because in this time, God is going to prepare you to be able to accept, sustain, and thrive in what is meant to be your end goal. Whether that end goal is a lifetime relationship with your partner, your purpose, or to gain a better perspective on life, God is preparing you for it and the sooner you develop this perspective of what you are going through as being necessary, the sooner you will stop living your life in a constant state of uncertainty, doubt, and fear, and instead start to live your life with, certainty, trust, and belief—which will enable you to live with happiness, peace, and joy.

Many of us wake up every day in a negative space because we live with stress, worry, and fear about the position we are currently in. We don't understand the season we are in at this very moment. We use comparison as a way to hurt ourselves even more by looking at another person's season and saying to ourselves, *they are rich and happy, but I am struggling to make ends meet. Their business is doing a million dollars in sales and yet mine is barely covering operating costs. He is already a professional boxer and I am still training to become one. He is an award-winning author and I am still working on my books.* You're not alone in this. I too was guilty of comparing my season with someone else's, which made me question God and his plan for me. But what I didn't understand then and what you don't understand now is that God created us with our own unique purpose, which means our journey to our purpose is also going to be a unique one. Therefore, don't look at someone else's season and start to lose faith, because you might be judging their winning season over your growing season. Through faith, you have to understand that when you're ready for what is yours, God will give it to you—but only when he knows you can accept it, sustain it, and thrive in it.

I am currently in a season of learning to always be my conscious, loving, and kind self, and it is one of the most difficult things I have been through in life, because God keeps sending me people and situations that push my buttons. Without having the perspective of understanding my current season of growth through faith, I would certainly live as many of you are living right now: with fear, uncertainty, and doubt. However, I understand my season and I know God is wanting me to learn to always be myself regardless of what is taking place so that when my dream of having a platform comes, I will be ready to bring my true self to that platform. I know this and I understand it, therefore I never have thoughts of worry, fear, and doubt about the position I am in right now; I just know what I am going through is necessary.

Now imagine yourself going through a difficult season in your life; would you have the perspective of understanding that season, no matter how good or bad it is? The reason I want you to understand your season of life is because your life is going to have many growing seasons, and if you don't understand why you are going through them, you will live in a suffering space. Just imagine if you didn't learn that God is putting you in difficult times not to break you but to build you. Those bad relationships he keeps putting you in will start to seem like repeated acts of torture. After that fifth one, you would just be fed up and start to play the victim card by believing, *Life is out to get me, why me? I have done nothing wrong. I don't deserve this.* You will then move into a negative state, because you think life is unfair and is out to get you and only you. With no perspective of understanding your season, you will live your days with unhappiness, worry, and stress. But imagine if you understood that God is putting you in those relationships so you can learn to have self-respect for yourself, so that when your dream man or dream woman walks into your life you will know how to act in that relationship in order to accept it, sustain it, and thrive in it. Going through that difficult season would be a lot easier if you understood why you are going through it. If you always understand the seasons God puts you in, whether they are good or bad, you will always live with more peace, happiness, and joy, but many people do not do this, and these are the people who suffer every single day by reacting negatively to their season. These people need to listen to Joel Osteen, who said, "The enemy always fights you hardest when he knows God has something great in your future." When you develop this perception of always understanding your season, when hard times arise you will also understand that good things are around the corner. When you understand this, you will not live in a state of suffering while waiting for those good things to come; you will just live with faith, which will allow you to live with more peace and happiness.

I know this can be hard to accept; sometimes even I question God and his plan for me. I was recently in a season of being addicted to pornography. I hated being in this position and I didn't understand why God put me in it. I felt so weak

79

caving to these desires and every time I did, I hated myself for it. I spent much time questioning God and losing my faith in him until one day I sat alone and realized that one of the things I asked God to allow me to do as my end goal was to create a beautiful family with the person I am with right now. Through prayer he said, *When I give you the platform, money, and fame, these impulses you see online will come into reality by women constantly throwing themselves at you, because of what you have. If you want to able to sustain the relationship I have given you, you need to be able to control your impulses, so that is what I am teaching you in this difficult time.* I finally understand that God is putting me in this situation of being addicted to pornography so that he can teach me to not react to my impulses so that when my platform, fame, and success come, I will be able to remain faithful in my relationship. I share this with you because I know many of you have asked God for an end goal, but when he puts you in difficult times to see if you can accept, sustain, and thrive in your end goal, you start to question his character and plan for you. We all need to learn to react to our difficult times with acceptance and a mind frame of understanding instead of anger, frustration, and negativity. That way, when the difficult times arise in your life, whether in the form of a tough relationship, your business going through the startup stages, or finding yourself in a period of depression, you can respond to these situations with acceptance and understanding rather than fear, doubt, and worry.

Always understand the season you are in. Always understand that when your purpose is bigger than yourself God will help you. Always see the silver lining in what you are going through, by understanding that there is a reason behind your difficult time. When you put all of these things together and through faith understand your seasons, you will begin to live with nirvana—unshakable peace. I no longer react with anger to those people and situations that are testing me; I smile now, because I know God is sending them to me for a reason. He is putting me through this difficult time for a reason. The minute you have the thought, *the difficult time in my life right now is necessary for my end goal,* you instantly feel lighter and happier. No matter what life throws at you or what you go through, you will understand it. When you get to this stage, nothing life puts you through will be able to shake your inner peace, happiness, and joy.

The reason I shared these three points with you is to encourage people all across the world to live with faith. I know that when I started to live with faith, I stopped living every day with fear, uncertainty, stress, doubt, and worry. I would wake up and be scared of the future, thinking, *are people really going to listen to me? Are people really going to love my book? What if my girlfriend leaves me? What if my family dies? What if my purpose never comes into fruition?* These questions of uncertainty cause us to live in a suffering state. Faith allows you to live your everyday life with peace of mind, because at the end of the day there is no point in worrying, being afraid, or by having anxiety about the things you simply cannot control.

If we dissect our thoughts through awareness, we can come to the realization that most of what we stress and worry about is out of our control anyway. I can't control how many people read my book; I can only control writing the best book that I can possibly write. I can't control when my family members die, but I can control making beautiful memories with them until their time is up. I can't control my girl-friend's character, but I can control my behavior and being the best possible human I can be for her.

This isn't about ignoring your problems or thinking that if you have faith, everything will take care of itself. No, that is not the point at all, because faith without work is nonexistent. You still need to work extremely hard at the things you can control, but for the things that are beyond you, all that's needed is faith. Learn to harbor faith and use it to eliminate stress, anxiety, and fear over the things that you cannot control. Give up control! Realize that you can't control everything, and be okay with that, because when you are is when you will reach a level of peace that cannot be disrupted; that is when you will live your days with true peace, happiness, and joy.

You Versus You

These teachings are not intended to be about escaping to a time when things seem better. They are instead about going through life now and learning to deal with the hindrances that arise in your life, whether that is fear, suffering or pain. These teachings are about finding the pleasure in the moments we are currently experiencing. They are about being happy during the chaos. They aren't about not suffering during the storm of debt, depression, and setbacks. They are instead about learning to live in a nirvana state throughout all the seasons of life. These teachings are not about running away until life gets better, because we never know when better will come or what it will look like. We don't know what life will give us and at what time, which is why we have to live life as the same in every moment. There are no such things as bad or good moments, because a blessing never looks like a blessing in the moment. My reason for teaching you this is because I want you to live as yourself through all the moments of your life.

As you continue to practice this new way of living—defining who you want to be, plucking your thoughts, meditating, finding pleasure in your simple moments, and having faith—you will begin to realize that there are two of you: your conscious self and your unconscious self. One of you is the person you are, which is made up of your old unconscious habits; and the other is the person who you want to be. The one that you continuously act like will grow while the other one fades away. Therefore, to be your new self you need to develop the discipline to act as that person every day. When you do this, you will develop the habit of always being yourself. It is a habit to constantly breathe through your nose to ground your helium balloon of a mind. It is a habit to constantly remind yourself to be in loving kindness. It is a habit to pluck your thoughts. It is a habit to remind yourself to have faith. It is a habit to remind yourself to find pleasure in your simple moments. It is a constant habit to be aware and conscious.

When I started to do these six things—defining who I want to be, plucking my thoughts, meditating, finding pleasure in my simple moments, and having faith—I felt so much happier, and the reason for my happiness weighed heavily on the fact that I loved myself. I loved who I was. I loved how I treated people in reality and in my mind. I loved how I could instantly change my mood by plucking my thoughts. I loved how I lived with certainty and trust over fear and worry. Most of all, I loved how my mind was a beautiful place to live in. However, to be this person it took and still takes a constant effort and battle to fight the old me. At times, it feels as if I am bipolar and caught between the person I was and the person I want to be. One minute I was living my life in a state of clarity, but the next I was daydreaming about porn for two hours. To be yourself, it takes constant awareness and discipline whereas being your old self takes no awareness and no discipline. You may recognize why people choose the second option. But those people who choose the second option don't realize that they are creating their future self through the way they live today. I understand, and I want you to as well so that when your old self tries slipping through the cracks, you are conscious and disciplined enough to continue to be yourself even though it may be easier to be your old self. Live with sustained awareness of yourself, in which you know the difference between the you that you are being, and always have the discipline to pick growth over comfort. It will always be comfortable to act as your old self, which is why most people never change. To be the person you want to be, you need to practice being that person; the more you practice, the more natural being this person will become. To live as yourself, it takes constant awareness so remind yourself how to live. Take breaks throughout the day and sit and just breathe in order to ground your mind. Take a moment to remind yourself to act in loving kindness. Remind yourself when you're overthinking to pluck your thoughts. Remind yourself to breathe in all your moments, so you can be present in them.

Living with yourself truly means you are happy and at peace with the person you are. You are at peace and happy with the way you treat yourself and others. You are happy and at peace with the way you act and think every day. You are happy and at peace with the way you respond to life. You are happy and at peace every waking moment of your life. Once you are happy and at peace by learning to live with yourself you yourself have created nirvana – unshakeable peace. To live as yourself, you will need to have sustained awareness and discipline over yourself, but I promise you that your life will be filled with more peace, happiness, and joy than ever before. The greatest gift that you can give to yourself, and to the people around you, is to live to be able to *live with yourself*.

Sources

Allen, James, et al. The James Allen Collection: As a Man
    Thinketh; All These Things Added; The Way of Peace;
    Above Life's Turmoil; The Eight Pillars of Prosperity.
    Bottom of the Hill Publishing, 2010. Pg. 20, 22

"Anthony Ray Hinton Featured on 60 Minutes." Equal Justice
    Initiative, 9 Dec. https://eji.org/news/anthony-ray-hinton-
    on-60-minutes/. Pg. 56

Chödrön, Pema. *When Things Fall Apart: Heart Advice for Difficult
    Times.* Thorsons Classics, 2017. Pg. 71, 72

Dispenza, Joe. "The Art of Change." Dr. Joe Dispenza's Blog,
    10 June 2019, drjoedispenza.net/blog/the-art-of-change/ Pg. 6

Dispenza, Joe, and Daniel G. Amen. *Breaking the Habit of Being
    Yourself: How to Lose Your Mind and Create a New One.* Hay
    House, 2015. Pg. 19

Dyer, Wayne W. "Why the Inside Matters." *Dr. Wayne W. Dyer,*
    18 July 2017, www.drwaynedyer.com/blog/why-the-inside-
    matters/. Pg. 46

"Five Hindrances." Wikipedia, Wikimedia Foundation, 10 Nov.
    2020, en.m.wikipedia.org/wiki/Five hindrances. Pg. 22

McDonald, Kathleen. *How to Meditate,* Wisdom Publications,
    1984. Printed with permission from Wisdom Publications,
    www.wisdompubs.org. Pg. 33, 34, 35

Randolph, Marc. "Inside Netflix's Crazy, Doomed Sales Pitch to
    Blockbuster." Vanity Fair, 19 Sept. 2019, www.vanityfair.com/
    news/2019/09/netflixs-crazy-doomed-meeting-with-block-
    buster. Pg. 73

Acknowledgments

Thank you to my brother Sunny for going through life first so you could teach us from your mistakes and successes. Thank you to my brother Mike—*"Remember nobody believed in us when they see us now, they can't believe it's us."* —*Meek Mill.* Thank you to my Mom and Dad, I love you guys and all that you have done for me, putting a roof over my head, clothes on my back, food on the table and never charging us rent. You two are the reason your kids can chase their dreams—I hope you never forget that. You are my best friends and I love you more than life itself. Thank you to my Nana and Nani who made our family a happier one. Thank you Anita for being an amazing human being, who helped me find myself and loved me even when I did not know who I was or loved myself. Thank you to my nieces Journey and Story, who keep filling my life with laughter, joy and happiness. Thank you to my sister Dom for providing beautiful memories and being the best dance partner. Thank you to Sunita, Raj and Mum for all the beautiful memories we have created, you guys make my life more enjoyable. Thank you to my cousin Gavin who made my years at work a memorable experience, I will always cherish the memories we had at elm house. Thank you to my future children, you guys are the reason why I do what I do, so I can show you what it means to live your wildest dreams.

Notes

Notes

Notes

Notes

Notes

Notes

Notes

Notes

Notes

Notes

Notes

CPSIA information can be obtained
at www.ICGtesting.com
Printed in the USA
LVHW091137190521
687799LV00001B/2/J